RESOLVING DEVELOPMENTAL POLICY CONTROVERSIES

RESOLVING DEVELOPMENTAL POLICY CONTROVERSIES

STUART S. NAGEL

Nova Science Publishers, Inc.
Huntington, New York

Editorial Production:	Susan Boriotti
Office Manager:	Annette Hellinger
Graphics:	Frank Grucci and Jennifer Lucas
Information Editor:	Tatiana Shohov
Book Production:	Donna Dennis, Patrick Davin, Christine Mathosian, Tammy Sauter and Lynette Van Helden
Circulation:	Maryanne Schmidt
Marketing/Sales:	Cathy DeGregory

Library of Congress Cataloging-in-Publication Data

Resolving developmental policy controversies / Stuart S. Nagel, ed..
                           p.   cm.
       Includes index.
       ISBN 1-56072-739-X
       1. Developing countries--Economic policy--Decision making. 2. Policy sciences. I. Nagel,
Stuart S., 1934-
HC59.7.R472   1999   99-051428
320.6--dc21   CIP

Copyright 2000 by Nova Science Publishers, Inc.
       227 Main Street, Suite 100
       Huntington, New York 11743
       Tele. 631-462-6682   Fax 631-462-4666
       e-mail: Novascience@earthlink.net
       e-mail: Novascil@aol.com
       Web Site: http://www.nexusworld.com/nova

Printed in the United States of America

CONTENTS

LIST OF TABLES

Chapter 1

BASIC METHODS AND CONCEPTS

I. AN OUTLINE OF PUBLIC POLICY ANALYSIS

A. PUBLIC POLICY
   1. Government
       a.   All Branches: Legislative, Executive, and Judicial
       b.   All levels: International, National, Provincial, and Local
   2. Decision-Making
       a.   Over Time
       b.   Across Cases
   3. For Dealing With
       a.   Subjects in which the government is not involved
       b.   Subsidies
       c.   Private Litigation
       d.   Regulation
       e.   Ownership
   4. Societal Problems
       a.   Economic
       b.   Social
       c.   Political
       d.   Technological
       e.   International
       f.   Legal
B. POLICY ANALYSIS
   1. General
       a.   Nature
       b.   Causes
       c.   Effects
   2. Elements of Systematic Evaluation
       a.   Goals
       b.   Alternatives

        c. Relations

        d. Conclude Tentatively

        e. What-If Analysis

    3. When

        a. Pre-Adoption

        b. Post-Adoption

    4. By Whom

        a. Policy-Makers

        b. Policy-Analysis

        c. Policy-Appliers

C. INSTITUTION BUILDING

    1. Definition

        a. Procedures

        b. Facilitators

    2. Institutions

        1. Universities

        2. Independent Institutes

        3. Government Agencies

    3. Activities

        a. Training

        b. Research and Consulting

        c. Publishing

        d. Funding

        e. Networking and Associations

D. OTHER IMPORTANT CONCEPTS

    1. Feasibility

        a. Economics

        b. Political (Adoption)

        c. Constitutional or Legal

        d. Administrative (Implementation)

        e. Technological

        f. Psychological

    2. Spreadsheet-Table Analysis

    3. Super-Optimizing

        a. Exceeding Conservative Alternative on Conservative Goals

        b. Exceeding Liberal Alternative on Liberal Goal

        c. Substantial Exceeding

        d. Capable of Adoption

        e. Capable of Implementation

    4. Relation Scores (Alternatives and Goals)

        5 = **

        4 = *

        3 = 0

        2 = -

1 = --
5. Weights of Goals Relatively
    3 = Highly Important
    2 = Middling Important
    1 = Low Important

II. WHAT IS IMPROVED POLICY ANALYSIS?

Improved or contemporary policy analysis can be defined as systematically processing a set of societal goals to be achieved, policy alternatives available for achieving them, and relations between goals and alternatives in order to arrive at or explain a best alternative, combination, or allocation of scarce resources. That kind of policy analysis (which is becoming increasingly prevalent in the 1990s) differs from more traditional policy analysis in various ways.[1]

Those differences include:

1. On the one hand, much of the traditional policy analysis tends to be ideological in the sense that many policy analysts in Eastern Europe and China would choose among alternatives by asking which is the most communist, socialist, or Marxist.[2] Policy analysts in Western Europe and the United States would choose among alternatives by asking which is the most capitalist, private-enterprise oriented, or in the best interests of western nationalism.[3]

---

[1] On improved policy analysis, see Edward Quade, Analysis for Public Decision (North-Holland, 1988); John Mullen and Byron Roth, Decision Making: Its Logic and Practice (Rowman and Littlefield, 1991); John Arnold, The Art of Decision Making (American Management Associations, 1978); S. Nagel, Professional Developments in Policy Studies (Greenwood Press, 1992); and S. Nagel, Developing Nations and Super-Optimum Policy Analysis (Nelson-Hall, 1992).

[2] On socialistic policy analysis, see Michael Harrington, Why We Need Socialism in America (Dissent, 1971); and Paul Sweezy, Socialism (McGraw-Hill, 1949). On the China population problem, see Judith Banister, China's Changing Population (Stanford University Press, 1987); and Jean Robinson, "Of Family Policies in China" from Richard Hula and Elaine Anderson (eds.), The Family and Public Policy (Greenwood press, 1991)

[3] On capitalistic policy analysis, see Milton Friedman, Capitalism and Freedom (University of Chicago Press, 1963); and George Gilder, Wealth and Poverty (Basic books, 1980). On land reform and agricultural policy as it pertains to developing countries, see William Browne and Don Hadwiger (eds.), World Food Policies: Toward Agricultural Independence (Lynne 1986); John Mellor, "Agriculture on the Road to Industrialization" in John Lewis and Laleriana Kallab (eds.), Development Strategies Reconsidered (Transaction Books, 1986); and Raid El-Ghonemy, The Political Economy of Rural Poverty: The Case of Land Reform (Routledge, Chapman, and Hall, 1991).

2. On the other hand, almost as an over-reaction to ideology, many traditional policy analysts tended to go overboard in a *technocratic* or mathematical direction. They would seek to choose among alternative policies through statistical analysis or deductive models which often concentrated on relatively unimportant choices because the data was more available or measurable.
3. The new policy analysis tends to be sensitive to the *equity* and fairness goals of the ideological analysis while at the same time making use of *relevant quantitative methods*.

More specifically, the new policy analysis tends to use methods which emphasize the following:

1. *Multiple goals*, rather than single objective functions. Those multiple goals include conservative, liberal, and neutral goals. They may be measured in a variety of ways, not just in terms of dollars.
2. *Multiple alternatives*, rather than just go/no-go decisions. The go/no-go decision tends to be associated with probabilistic decision theory which is highly mathematical, and with the verbalizing of pro-con analysis associated with non-quantitative thinkers going back at least to Benjamin Franklin in American history.
3. Relations between multiple goals and multiple alternatives that allow for missing *information*, with variations on break-even analysis for making decisions without complete information. The relations also tend to be measured on simple scales like 1-5 scales so that scores can be indicated for virtually every relation without demanding unnecessary quantification.
4. The idea of multiple goals, multiple alternatives, and variations on break-even or what-if analysis logically leads to the increasing uses of multi-criteria decision making and *spreadsheet-based* decision-aiding software. This can be contrasted with less useful methods that emphasize linear programming, decision trees, and calculus curves.
5. The new policy analysis also shows more concern for what to do after a policy is recommended. That means a concern for the practical aspects of getting the policy *adopted and successfully implemented*. It thus means a concern for political, economic, administrative, and constitutional feasibility.
6. An especially exciting recent development involves getting away from thinking in terms of tradeoffs and compromises and instead thinking in terms of *super-optimum solutions* whereby conservatives, liberals, and other major viewpoints can all come out ahead of their best expectations simultaneously.

The above concepts are useful but too abstract in themselves without concrete applications from the real world of public policy-making. Two such sets of applications can be used for illustrative purposes of the nature and need for improved policy analysis. One application relates to population control in China.

III. INSTITUTIONALIZING IMPROVED POLICY ANALYSIS

It is one thing to talk about the desirability of super-optimizing policy analysis. It is another thing to talk about establishing or improving a set of institutions for more effectively arriving at super-optimum solutions in public policy analysis. The discussion below is also applicable to institutionalizing improved policy analysis that seeks to find the best alternative, combination, or allocation among various alternatives without necessarily arriving at super-optimum solutions.[4]

Table 1.1 is entitled, "Institutions for Policy Studies Activities." There are five activities listed on the columns, consisting of training, research, funding, publishing, and associations. There are three basic institutions listed along the rows, consisting of universities, independent institutes or private-sector entities, and government agencies. There are also three basic concepts on the lower rows, consisting of trends, examples from developing nations, and SOS solutions for synthesizing the work of the three basic institutions on each of the five policy analysis activities.

---

[4] On institutionalizing policy analysis (including training, research, funding, publishing, and networking institutions), see John Crecine, The New Educational Programs in Public Policy: The First Decade (JAI Press, 1982); Ilene Bernstein and Howard Freeman, Academic and Entrepreneurial Research: The Consequences of Diversity in Federal Evaluation Studies (Russell Sage, 1975); Virginia White, Grants: How To Find Out About Them and What To Do Next (Plenum, 1975); Carolyn Mullins, A Guide to Writing and Publishing in the Social and Behavioral Sciences (Wiley, 1977); UNESCO, International Organizations in the Social Sciences (UNESCO, 1981); and S. Nagel, The Policy Studies Handbook (Lexington-Heath, 1980).

TABLE 1.1 INSTITUTIONS FOR POLICY STUDIES ACTIVITIES

Activities / Institutions and concepts	1. Training (3 Tracks)	2. Research (3 Tracks)	3. Funding (for training and research)	4. Publishing (books and journals)	5. Associations (mutual interactions)
A. Universities	Career preparation	Generalized or basic research	1. Career training 2. Basic research	University presses Scholarly journals	Scholarly associations
B. Independent Institutes and Private Sector	Continuing policy education (CPE)	Intermediate or mid-level research (Evaluation research)	1. Continuing education 2. Mid-level research	Commercial publishing Commercial journals	Interest groups
C. Government Agencies	Job-specific (OJT)	Task-specific (Program evaluation)	1. Job-specific 2. Task-specific	Internal reports Internal periodicals	Government agencies
D. Trends	70s schools 80s texts 90s CPE	70s centers 80s texts 90s CPE	70s up 80s down 90s ?	70s new 80s plateau 90s plateau	70s new 80s plateau 90s plateau
E. Developing Nations	e.g., Beijing U. NSA Ministry of Electronics	e.g., Zambia U. CAFRAD UN Commission	e.g., MUCLA Ford Foundation AID and World Bank	e.g., Macmillan PSO journals	e.g., EROPA UN-USA PRC
F. SOS Solutions	All	All	All	All	All

A. Five Policy Analysis Activities and Three Institutions

The first column deals with *training*. The cells within each column emphasize what each institution can do best on the activity that is associated with the column. On the matter of training, universities are best on career preparation. That includes university programs in public policy, public administration, political science, or another social science where the program is geared toward training practitioners or academics who will spend a substantial amount of their time evaluating alternative public policies or other forms of policy analysis. Government agencies are especially good at on-the-job training. An example would be a training program within the Department of Housing and Urban Development to teach policy analysts or other HUD employees how to evaluate applications for urban development grants or alternative public housing proposals. Independent entities refer to those which are neither universities nor government agencies. They can include the American Society for Public Administration conducting pre-conference workshops designed to upgrade the skills of governmental decision makers, or the American Bar Association conducting continuing legal education (CLE) programs. The abbreviation CPE for continuing policy education programs is used in the table.

The second column deals with *research* activities. The universities are especially oriented toward generalized or basic research. They are also most appropriate if one wants to emphasize innovative creativity. In-house government research is especially effective for more specific tasks from an insider's perspective. It is research that has a good chance of being adopted, just as on-the-job training (OJT) has a good chance of leading to a higher job. The independent institutes range from high-quality policy institutes like the Brookings Institution and the American Enterprise Institute to institutes that are sometimes referred to as beltway bandits who specialize in good packaging but possibly shallow substance at high prices. The independent institutes do well on complying with time and subject-matter specifications.

The third column is concerned with *funding* activities. Much of the policy training and research at universities is funded internally through legislative appropriations, alumni contributions, and student tuition, but also from government grants and foundations. The independent sector can include policy institutes and also funding sources like the Ford Foundation. Both may benefit from endowments. Most independent institutes, however, rely on soft money and they usually do better financially on business training and research than on governmental training and research. The government agencies tend to rely almost exclusively on taxes to fund their training and research activities. They could rely more on the willingness of many academics to participate in training and research activities for only the out-of-pocket cost, in view of the interest of policy academics in insightful experiences and in making a worthwhile contribution.

The fourth column relates to *publishing* as a policy studies activity, including both books and journals. Universities provide university presses, which publish some policy-relevant books, although they tend to be concerned with more abstract matters or more geographically-narrow matters. Some universities publish relevant scholarly journals, such as the *Policy Studies Journal* and the *Policy Studies Review* which have been published at various universities since they began. The private sector publishes policy-relevant books series, such as those published by Ashgate, Greenwood, Macmillan, JAI Press, Marcel Dekker, Lexington, Sage, and others. Many of the relevant journals are commercially published, such as the *Journal of Policy Analysis and Management*, which is published by Wiley Publishers. Government agencies do relevant publishing in the form of internal reports and internal periodicals. The U.S. Government Accounting Office does both.

The fifth column deals with *associations* as forms of mutual interaction and networking. People at universities tend to be associated with scholarly associations, such as the American Political Science Association (APSA) or the Policy Studies Organization (PSO). The private sector tends to be organized into interest groups that take a strong interest in public policy, such as the various trade and professional associations. The private sector also includes public-interest groups like Common Cause or more partisan groups like the Americans for Democratic Action. People from government agencies often belong to specialized associations which might emphasize public works, criminal justice, or education. They also join more general practitioner groups which also include academics like the American Evaluation Association (AEA) or the American Society for Public Administration (ASPA).

B. Trends, Developing Nations, and SOS

On the matter of *trends*:

1. Training in the 70's emphasized the development of new schools like the Kennedy School of Government at Harvard or the Graduate School of Public Policy at Berkeley. The 80's emphasized the development of new public policy textbooks, starting with books by Edward Quade or the Rand Corporation and by Edith Stokey and Richard Zechkauser of the Harvard Kennedy School. The 90's may see more emphasis on continuing policy education with the upgrading of skills through workshops and OJT, as in other industries.
2. Research in the 70's emphasized the establishment of research centers like the American Enterprise Institute. The 80's saw an outpouring of books from such centers, as well as other sources such as the Policy Studies Organization. The 90's are seeing more research and publishing that is relevant to providing materials for continuing policy education, rather than so much emphasis on textbooks and trade-books.
3. Trends in funding included being upward in the 70's when money was more readily available for policy research from the Carter administration, but downward in the 80's when it was less available from the Reagan administration. The 90's may see an increase in policy analysis funding as part of the peace dividend and the increased interest in industrial policy and the role of the government in stimulating the marketplace.

4. There were new journals in the 70's including *PSJ, PSR*, and *JPAM*. There has been leveling-off in the 80's, although at a high level. That is likely to continue in the 90's.
5. Associations tend to be related to journals. The 70's saw new policy associations established, such as PSO, APPAM, and AEA. There has been a leveling-off in the 80's and 90's. One upsurge, though, has been the expansion of policy associations toward being more cross-national. The Policy Studies Organization has thus established regional PSO's in Asia, Africa, East Europe, and Latin America.

The above analysis has tended to use American examples. We could discuss each of the five activities in terms of examples from *developing nations*, such as:

1. Policy analysis training in China as elsewhere involves universities, independent institutes, and government agencies. Beijing University has an excellent program in foreign policy and international relations. National School of Administration is a semi-independent training institute which has links with People's University and also the government. A good example of in-house government training is the Ministry of Machinery and Electronics which has its own training campus.
2. One can use Africa to illustrate the role of universities, institutes, and government agencies in research. Zambia University in the Political Science Department does policy-relevant research on electoral reform and other matters. The African Training and Research Center in Administration for Development (CAFRAD) is a policy institute which does excellent research and publishing on African policy problems. A relevant government agency might be the United Nations Economic Commission on Africa, or the Commonwealth Secretariat. Both also encourage relevant conferences and research.
3. Funding for training and research in developing nations includes university programs like the Midwest University Consortium for International Affairs (MUCIA). Good examples of the semi-private sector funding training and research are the Ford, the Asia, and Rockefeller Foundations. Important government agencies include the Agency for International Development and the World Bank. Both have recently taken an increased interest in the importance of democratic institutions and systematic public policy analysis.
4. There are a number of book publishers who have specialized series that deal with developing nations, such as Macmillan, M. E. Sharpe, and Kumerian. There are many journals that specialize in developing nations, such as the *Journal of Commonwealth and Comparative Politics*, the *Journal of Asian Studies*, the *Journal of Development Studies and African Affairs*, and the *Latin American Research Review*.
5. An example of a scholarly association concerned with developing nations is the Eastern Regional Organization of Public Administration. It is the Asia regional organization for the International Association of Schools and Institutes of Administration. A relevant interest group is the UN-USA. It is an American

organization that supports the activities of the United Nations including activities directed toward economic, social, technological, political, and legal development. An example of a government agency in a developing nation context might be the PRC Ministry of Foreign Affairs, which seeks to bring students to China from developing nations of Africa and elsewhere in Asia.

The last row of the table addresses the question of what is a super-optimum way of resolving the division of labor between universities, independent private institutes, and government agencies, in dealing with policy training, research, funding, publishing, and associations. One could say that emphasizing the private sector is the conservative way. Emphasizing government agencies is the liberal way. Emphasizing universities is relatively neutral, although some universities are governmental and some are private. The super-optimum solution is not a compromise that involves giving more to the neutral position. That would defeat the purpose of getting the separate benefits of each type of institution. Rather, the SOS solution seeks to expand the policy activities of universities, independent institutes, and government agencies all simultaneously. There is plenty of room for that kind of three-way expansion, given the need for better policy analysis in order to have better public policies and a better quality of life in industrial and developing nations. That means more and better policy training, research, funding, publishing, and associations through universities, independent institutes and government agencies.[5]

IV. SOME INTEGRATING CONCLUSIONS

Some of the *integrating ideas* that are relevant to this chapter on the need for improved policy analysis in developing regions are:

1. Improved policy analysis involves the ability to deal with multiple goals, multiple alternatives, missing information, spreadsheet-based decision-aiding software, a concern for successful adoption and implementation, and the striving for super-optimum solutions whereby conservatives, liberals, and other major

---

[5] For additional literature on the subject of capacity building regarding policy analysis institutions in developing nations, see Edward Jaycox, The African Capacity Building Initiative: Toward Improved Policy Analysis and Development Management in Sub-Saharan Africa (The World Bank, 1991); Mohan Kaul and Gelase Mutahaba, Enhancement of Public Policy Management Capacity in Africa (Commonwealth Secretariat and African Association for Public Administration and Management, 1991); Vasant Moharir, "Capacity Building Initiative for Sub-Saharan Africa," in J. Pronk (ed.), Sub-Saharan Africa: Beyond Adjustment (Netherlands Ministry of Foreign Affairs, 1990). For additional literature on the subject of allocating scarce resources among alternative activities, see S. Nagel, "Allocating Scarce Resources," in Decision-Aiding Software: Skills, Obstacles and Applications (Macmillan, 1991); and S. Nagel, "Super-Optimum Solutions and Allocation Problems," in Policy Analysis Methods, Process, and Super-Optimum Solutions (Greenwood, 1992).

viewpoints can all come out ahead of their best initial expectations simultaneously.

2. Improved policy analysis requires more than a systematic analytic methodology. It also requires a system of institutions like universities, independent institutes, and government agencies performing essential functions with regard to training, research, funding, publishing, and networking.

On a higher level of integration, there is a need to emphasize more the *mutual interdependence* of effective policy analysis methods and effective policy analysis institutions:

1. The development of a methodology that is capable of determining an optimum or even a super-optimum alternative, combination, or allocation does not mean much unless the following activities are also occurring:

    (1) The methodology is being taught to students who are preparing for careers that involve policy analysis. It is also being taught to practitioners who have already gone beyond their college training.

    (2) The methodology is being applied in systematically evaluating alternative public policies that relate to economic, social, technological, political, and legal problems.

    (3) Funding is available to conduct the relevant training and the relevant research.

    (4) Books and journals are being published to facilitate the training activities by way of developing teaching materials. Books and journals are also being published to disseminate the results of the research and to share experiences on how future research and teaching can be improved.

    (5) Associations hold regular meetings in which papers are presented and roundtable discussions are held to indicate what is happening at the cutting-edge of policy analysis activities and also to establish mutually beneficial collaborative contacts.

2. The development of strong institutions with good potential for training, research, funding, publishing, and associations does not mean much if systematic policy analytic methodologies are not also being simultaneously developed. Otherwise:

    (1) The training programs will have nothing meaningful to teach or at least less than the optimum which they could be teaching.

    (2) The research activities are not so likely to develop results that are as insightful as they otherwise could be.

    (3) Much of the funding may be wasted on largely irrelevant or ineffective training and research.

    (4) The publishing may go through the motions of generating books and journals, but policy analysts who are academics or practitioners may be disappointed regarding how little value the books and journals might have.

    (5) The papers presented at associational meetings might overemphasize number crunching, unrealistic mathematical models, unnecessary jargon, and other

forms of modern scholasticism which have afflicted many professional associations. This is contrasted to a concern for dealing in a meaningful way with many important goals and alternatives in order to arrive at super-optimum or other conclusions which are relevant to improving the quality of life through better public policy in developing regions.

Perhaps the reciprocal nature of policy analysis methods and policy analysis institutions may seem obvious. Nevertheless, one can find important *literature that may over-emphasize* one at the expense of the other. For example, the publications of the World Bank, the Commonwealth Secretariat, and the African Association for Public Administration and Management on the subject of African capacity building may overemphasize building institutions without an adequate concern for building analytic methods. The methodology books, on the other hand, almost never talk about policy analysis institutions. The classic volumes by Edward Quade of the Rand Corporation, or Edith Stokey and Richard Zeckhauser of the Harvard Kennedy School have a lot to say about variations on management science, operations research, and decision analysis, but there is no mention in those books about training methods, research utilization, funding sources, publishing outlets, or relevant associations.

Perhaps the title of this section should be expanded to be "The Need for Improved Policy Analysis Methods and Institutions in Developing Nations and Elsewhere." More important than the title is the idea that there are these needs. It is hoped that this chapter will be a step in the direction toward clarifying and suggesting ways in which those needs can be met.

V. ALLOCATING $100 MILLION TO POLICY ANALYSIS ACTIVITIES AND INSTITUTIONS

The allocation *budget* of $100 million comes from page 27 of *The African Capacity Building Initiative: Toward Improved Policy Analysis and Development Management in Sub-Saharan Africa* (The World Bank, 1991). The exact quote is, "Financial resources will be needed to implement capacity building action programs . . . an ACB fund will be created initially of $100 million." See Table 1.2 entitled "Allocating World Bank Funds to Policy Analysis Activities and Institutions."

Training and research are given greater weight than funding, publishing, and associations since the second set of activities mainly serve to facilitate the first set of activities. The $100 million is allocated to the five activities in proportion to their weights.

Going down each activity separately, each institution is scored using *relative scoring*. Such scoring involves first deciding which institution is (relatively speaking) the least important of the three types of institutions. It is given an anchor score of 1. One then scores the middling institution as being twice as important as the base and half as important as the most important institution unless a more precise scoring system is needed and is available.

TABLE 1.2 ALLOCATING WORLD BANK FUNDS TO POLICY ANALYSIS ACTIVITIES AND INSTITUTIONS

Activities / Institutions	1. Training (3 Tracks) W = 2	2. Research (3 Tracks) W = 2	3. Funding (for training and research) W = 1	4. Publishing (books and journals) W = 1	5. Associations (mutual interactions) W = 1	Allocations (across each row)
L Universities	Career preparation 4 (56% = $16)	Generalized or basic research 4 (56% = $16)	1. Career training 2. Basic research 4 (56% = $8)	1. University presses 2. Scholarly journals 1 (14% = $2)	Scholarly associations 4 (56% = $8)	(50% = $50)
C Independent Institutes and Private Sector	Continuing policy education (CPE) 1 (14% = $4)	Intermediate or mid-level research (Evaluation research) 1 (14% = $4)	1. Continuing education 2. Mid-level research 1 (14% = $2)	1. Commercial publishing 2. Commercial journals 4 (56% = $8)	Interest groups 2 (28% = $4)	(22% = $22)
N Government Agencies	Job-specific (OJT) 2 (28% = $8)	Task-specific (Program evaluation) 2 (28% = $8)	1. Job-specific 2. Task-specific 2 (28% = $4)	1. Internal reports 2. Internal periodicals 2 (28% = $4)	Government agencies 1 (14% = $2)	(26% = $26)
Totals (down each column)	7 (100% = $28)	7 (100% = $28)	7 (100% = $14)	7 (100% = $14)	7 (100% = $14)	(100% = $100)

Budget = $100 Million

Those relative scores are then converted to *part/whole percentages* by adding down to determine the total of each column. Then divide the score in each cell by the total score of the column. The decimal equivalents of those part/whole percentages are then multiplied by the total allocated to each activity in order to determine the dollar *allocations* for each type of institution on each activity.

The total dollar allocations for each type of institution are determined by adding across the five separate allocations. The total allocation percentages for each institution are determined by adding across the weighted percentages and dividing by the sum of the weights.

All dollar amounts in the table are million dollar amounts. Due to rounding to the nearest million dollars, the percentages may sometimes add to slightly more or less than 100%. The dollar amounts may also add to slightly more or less than $100, $28, or $14.

This allocation analysis is not meant to be final. It is meant to be a *stimulus to thinking* systematically about how (on a relatively high level of generality) $100 million might best be allocated to various activities and institutions for improving African capacity building, especially with regard to systematic public policy analysis.

This allocation analysis may not lend itself to an *SOS allocation* since all the goals are ideologically neutral. None of the goals are relatively conservative or relatively liberal. Thus the alternative institutions receive only one set of allocation percentages and amounts, rather than a conservative and liberal set that need to be exceeded. One can say that emphasizing universities is relatively liberal, and emphasizing private sector institutes is relatively conservative, with government agencies in the middle. One needs ideological goals as well as alternatives, however, in order to have an ideological controversy subject to a super-optimum solution as contrasted to an optimum solution. The latter finds the best allocation in light of the goals, alternatives, and relations with only one set of weights. The SOS solution finds an alternative that does better than the conservative alternative with conservative weights, and simultaneously does better than the liberal alternative with liberal weights.[6]

---

[6] For more recent general references to developing nations, see:
1. Fred Lazin, Samuel Aroni, and Yehuda Gradus (eds.), The Policy Impact of Universities in Developing Regions (Macmillan Press Ltd., 1998).
2. Joseph Weatherby and others, The Other World: Issues and Politics of the Developing World (Longman, 1997).
3. Robert Griffiths, Developing World (Dushkin Publishing Group, 1997).
4. Stuart Nagel and Miriam Mills, Developing Nations and Super-Optimum Policy Analysis (Nelson Hall, 1993).
5. Stuart Nagel (ed.), Policy Studies and Developing Nations (JAI Press, 1996).
6. The State in a Changing World (The World Bank, 1997).

VI. SUPER-OPTIMIZING

A. What is Super-Optimizing?

Super-optimizing analysis refers to dealing with public policy problems by finding an alternative that enables conservatives, liberals, and other major viewpoints to all come out ahead of their best initial expectations simultaneously.

Super-optimum solutions in public controversies involve solutions that exceed the best expectations of liberals and conservatives simultaneously. We are primarily concerned with public or governmental controversies, not controversies among private individuals such as marriage, consumer, employment, or other such disputes. We are, however, interested in controversies over what statutes, judicial precedents, or administrative regulations should be adopted governing marriage, consumer, employment, or other such relations.

An optimum solution is one that is best on a list of alternatives in achieving a set of goals. A super-optimum solution is one that is simultaneously best on two separate sets of goals. One set is a liberal set, and the second set is a conservative set. Both sets may share many or all of the same goals, but they are likely to differ in terms of the relative weights they give to the same goals.

B. SOS Contrasted with Other Types of Solutions

Solutions to public controversies can be classified in various ways. First there are super-optimum solutions in which all sides come out ahead of their initial best expectations, as mentioned above. At the opposite extreme is a super-malimum solution in which all sides come out worse than their worst initial expectations. That can be the case in a mutually destructive war, labor strike, or highly expensive litigation.

Pareto optimum solutions in which nobody comes out worse off and at least one side comes out better off. That is not a very favorable solution compared to a super-optimum solution. A Pareto malimum solution would be one in which nobody is better off and at least one side is worse off.

A win-lose solution where what one side wins the other side loses. The net effect is zero when the losses are subtracted from the gains. This is the typical litigation dispute when one ignores the litigation costs.

A lose-lose solution where both sides are worse off than they were before the dispute began. This may often be the typical litigation dispute, or close to it when one includes litigation costs. Those costs are often so high that the so-called winner is also a loser. That is also often the case in labor-management disputes that result in a strike, and even more so in international disputes that result in going to war.

The so-called win-win solution, at first glance this sounds like a solution where everybody comes out ahead. What it typically refers to though is an illusion since the parties are only coming out ahead relative to their worst expectations. In this sense, the plaintiff is a winner no matter what the settlement is because the plaintiff could have won

nothing if liability had been rejected at trial. Likewise, the defendant is a winner no
matter what the settlement is because the defendant could have lost everything the
plaintiff was asking for if liability had been established at trial. The parties are only
fooling themselves in the same sense that someone who is obviously a loser tells himself
he won because he could have done worse.

Super-optimum solutions are alternatives to public policy problems which can enable
conservatives, liberals, and other major viewpoints to all come out ahead of their best
initial expectations simultaneously. The purpose of this chapter is to clarify how to
generate, adopt, and implement such solutions.

C. Generating Super-Optimum Solutions

There are approximately eight different ways of arriving at super-optimum solutions.
They consist of the following:

1. Expanding the resources available. An example might include well-placed
    subsidies and tax breaks that would increase national productivity and thus
    increase the growth national product and income. Doing so would enable the tax
    revenue to the government to increase even if the tax rate decreases. That would
    provide for a lowering of taxes, instead of trying to choose between liberal and
    conservative ways of raising them. It would also provide for increasing both
    domestic and defense expenditures, instead of having to choose between the two.
2. Setting higher goals than what was previously considered the best while still
    preserving realism. An example might include the Hong Kong labor shortage
    with unemployment at only 1%. Hong Kong is faced with the seeming dilemma
    of having to choose between foregoing profits (by not being able to fill orders
    due to lack of labor) and opening the floodgates to mainland Chinese and
    Vietnamese (in order to obtain more labor). A super-optimum solution might
    involve adding to the labor force by way of the elderly, the disabled, and mothers
    of preschool children. Also by providing more and better jobs for those who are
    seasonally employed, part-time employed, full-time employed but looking for a
    second job, and full-time employed but not working up to their productive
    capacity.
3. Situations where one side can receive big benefits but the other side incurs only
    small costs. An example is in litigation where the defendant gives products that it
    makes. The products may have high market value to the plaintiff, but low
    variable or incremental cost to the defendant, since the defendant has already
    manufactured the products or can quickly do so.
4. Situations involving a third party benefactor which is usually a government
    agency. An example is government food stamps which allow the poor to obtain
    food at low prices, while farmers receive high prices when they submit the food
    stamps they have received for reimbursement. Another example is rent

supplements which allow the poor to pay low rents, but landlords receive even higher rents than they would otherwise expect.

5. Combining alternatives that are not mutually exclusive. An example is combining government-salaried legal-aid attorneys with volunteer attorneys. Doing so could give the best of both the public sector and private sector approach to legal services for the poor. Another example is combining (1) tax-supported higher education plus democratic admission standards with (2) contributions from alumni and tuition plus merit standards. Doing so results in universities that are better than pure government ownership or pure private enterprise.

6. Removing or decreasing the source of the conflict between liberals and conservatives, rather than trying to synthesize their separate proposals. An example would be concentrating on having a highly effective and acceptable birth control program to satisfy both the proponents and opponents of abortion, since abortions would then seldom be needed. Another example would be concentrating on a highly effective murder-reduction program to satisfy both the proponents and opponents of capital punishment. Such a murder-reduction program might emphasize gun control, drug medicalization, and reduction of violence socialization.

7. Developing a package of alternatives that would satisfy both liberal and conservative goals. An example is pretrial release where liberals want more arrested defendants released prior to trial, and conservatives want a higher rate of appearances in court without having committed a crime while released. The package that increases the achievement of both goals includes better screening, reporting in, notification, and prosecution of no-shows, as well as reduction of delay between arrest and trial.

8. Redefining the problem so as to clarify the shared goals which both the liberals and conservatives are seeking. In that sense, an SOS solution is one that produces increases on the goals favored by conservatives and also on the goals favored by liberals, which are normally thought of as inherently involving a tradeoff situation. A good example is the problem of jury size in which conservatives want smaller juries so as to make it easier to convict the guilty. Liberals want larger juries to make it more difficult to convict the innocent. An SOS solution might redefine the problem to be, "How to simultaneously increase the probability of convicting the guilty and decrease the probability of convicting the innocent." In other words, how to make juries more accurate on both convicting the guilty and acquitting the innocent. Allowing note-taking by jurors and requiring accessible videotaping may do much more for each of those goals than a complete victory for either side on the almost irrelevant problem of jury size.

D. Chinese Population Control as an Example

1. Ideology and Technocracy

As of the 1970's, the People's Republic of China was seeking to resolve public policy problems largely by consulting the ideological writings of Karl Marx, Mao Zedong, and their interpreters. As of the 1980's, government agencies in China were seeking to become more professional by way of the introduction of personnel management, financial administration, and other bureaucratic ideas from the West, some of which are actually a throwback to Confucius bureaucracy.

Thus ideology became offset by technocracy. What we were seeing may fit the classic Hegelian and Marxist dialectic of thesis, antithesis, and synthesis. Ideology represented the prevailing thesis in the 1970's, whereby population control might be analyzed by reading Marx and Mao. Technocracy represented the antithesis in the 1980's, whereby population control might be analyzed by reading biological literature.

The 1990's represent a super-optimum synthesis of the best, not the worst of both possible worlds. It may draw upon the idea of having goal-oriented values from the ideological thesis, as contrasted to rejecting values as being unscientific or not objective. Values and goals may be quite objective in the sense of being provable means to higher goals, or in the sense of proving that certain alternatives are more capable of achieving the goals than others.

The 1990's have also draw upon the idea of empirical proof based on observable consequences, rather than ideological labels of socialism or capitalism. It is empirical proof that also makes sense in terms of deductive consistency with what else is known about the world, rather than mindless technical number-crunching without thinking about how the results might fit common sense. Being technical does not necessarily mean being effective in getting the job done efficiently and equitably, which is what should really count in governmental decision-making.

The kind of synthesis which this refers to is a synthesis of goals to be achieved (the ideological element) and systematic methods for determining which alternative or alternatives most achieve those goals (the technical element). The true dialectic is dynamic not only in the sense that a thesis leads to an antithesis which leads to a higher level synthesis. It is also dynamic in the sense that a synthesis does not stagnate, but becomes a subsequent thesis to be re-synthesized by a new antithesis into a still higher level of analysis. There may be policy evaluation methods that are even more effective, efficient, and equitable.

Those are the methods that are hinted at in various places in this paper where super-optimum solutions are explicitly or implicitly mentioned. Such solutions enable conservatives, liberals, and other major viewpoints to all come out ahead of their best initial expectations simultaneously. Traditional optimizing involves finding the best alternative or alternatives in a set. SOS analysis involves finding an alternative that is better than what conservatives previously considered the best and simultaneously better than what liberals previously considered the best, using conservative and liberal values.

Table 1.3 Super-Optimizing Analysis Applied to the China Excess Population Problem

CRITERIA / ALTERNATIVES	C Goal Small Families	L Goal Reproduc- tive Free- dom	N Total (Neutral Weights)	L Total (Liberal Weights)	C Total (Conservative Weights)
C Alternative Strict One-Child Policy	4	2	12	10	14*
L Alternative Flexible on Family Size	2	4	12	14*	10
N Alternative One Child With Exceptions Allowed	3	3	12	12	12
S Alternative Remove Causes of Excess Children	5	5	20	20**	20**

NOTES:
1. Relevant causes of excess children in the China population context include:
   (1) The need for adult children to care for their elderly parents which could be better handled through social security and/or jobs for the elderly.
   (2) The need for extra children to allow for child mortality, which could be better handled through better child health care.
   (3) The need for male children in view of their greater value, which could be better handled through providing more opportunities for females.
   (4) The lack of concern for the cost of sending children to college, which could be better handled through a more vigorous program of recruiting rural children to college.
2. It is not a super-optimum solution to provide monetary rewards and penalties in this context because:
   (1) The monetary rewards for having fewer children enable a family to then have more children.
   (2) The monetary punishments for having more children stimulate a family to have still more children to provide offsetting income.
   (3) The monetary rewards and punishments are made meaningless by the simultaneous policies which are increasing prosperity in rural China.

* Conservative or liberal winner without considering the SOS.
** Conservative or liberal winner when the SOS is considered.

2. Alternatives, Goals, and Relations as Inputs

Table 1.3 is entitled "Super-Optimizing Analysis Applied to the China Excess Population Problem." Also see Table 1.4 which is a simplified SOS table entitled "Simplified Table on Population Problem." They can be used to illustrate what is meant by super-optimizing policy analysis where all major viewpoints can come out ahead of their best initial expectations The tables talk about excess population, rather than about the population problem. This is so because most of China's so-called population problem does not relate to a surplus of people, but rather to a shortage of production. Some of the population problem (at least in the short run) may, however, relate to a strain on China's current resources that can be lessened by lessening the number of consumers.

The alternatives are listed on the rows. The conservative alternative (in the sense of being the most regulatory) is to try to enforce a strict one-child policy. The liberal alternative (in the sense of allowing the most freedom) is to be completely flexible on family size. This is also possibly most in conformity with Marxist ideology which tends to view population control as a capitalistic idea designed to either increase the population of the poor (in order to have a reserve army of unemployed people) or to decrease the population of the poor (out of fear that the poor will overwhelm the middle class). Those two Marxist views tend to nullify each other possibly leading one to the conclusion that there is no Marxist view on population policy. The compromise position between conservative regulation and liberal freedom is to have a one-child policy, but with various exceptions such as allowing a second child if the first is a daughter, or allowing a second child among rural but not urban people.

Table 1.4. Simplified Table on Population Problem

GOALS / ALTERNATIVES	C Small families.	L Reproductive freedom.
C Strict one-child policy.	+	-
L flexible on family size.	-	+
N One child with exceptions allowed.	0	0
SOS OR WIN-WIN Remove causes of excess children.	++	++

One of the key goals is small families given the tremendous burden on the Chinese economy and government services of a billion people reproducing at a rate greater than about one child per family. Even one child per family would mean substantial short-run population growth. This would occur because people are living longer in China. If one simplifies the arithmetic by saying that if the 500 million males marry the 500 million females and have one child apiece within the next few years, then the population goes from a billion to 1.5 billion. That increase of half a billion is more people than every country of the world currently has with the exception of China and India. The rich may not get richer, but the highly populated get even more highly populated. The second key goal is reproductive freedom. Even the conservatives recognize that interfering with reproductive freedom makes for a lot of antagonism toward the government. Thus both goals are endorsed by both conservatives and liberals in China, but Chinese conservatives place relatively more emphasis on small families, and Chinese liberals place relatively more emphasis on reproductive freedom.

The relations between the alternatives and the goals are shown in Table 1.3 on a 1-5 scale where 5 means highly conducive to the goal, 4 means mildly conducive, 3 means neither conducive nor adverse, 2 means mildly adverse, and 1 means highly adverse to the goal. We have here a classic tradeoff even more so than the previous three tables. A strict one-child policy is good on small families, but bad on reproductive freedom. Flexibility on family size is good on reproductive freedom, but bad on small families. The compromise alternative is middling on both. Like compromises in general. This compromise is better than the worst on both small families and reproductive freedom. It is clearly not better than the best expectations on either goal.

3. Finding a Super-Optimum Package of Policies

In many public policy problems, the super-optimum solution involves well-placed subsidies and tax breaks. Well-placed tax breaks are meaningless in a communist society. Under communism, people do not do much direct tax-paying (especially income taxes) the way they do in western societies. Instead the government is supported by paying people less than they are worth in their government jobs. The difference is a hidden tax. Ironically this fits well the Marxist idea of surplus-value exploitation of labor. It is an easy, form of tax to collect, but it does not allow for the use of tax breaks as incentives.

China has tried subsidizing small families by giving monetary rewards to those who have small families, and monetary punishments to those who do not have them. The effect has been almost the opposite of the government's intent. The subsidies to small families have in many instances increased their income so they can now afford to have more children. Having a monetary punishment or reduced salary may even motivate parents to have an additional child to help bring in more income to offset the reduced salary. Also, moving simultaneously toward a more prosperous free market (especially in farm products) has enabled many rural people to now have more children and not be bothered by the withdrawal of subsidies or other monetary punishments.

A kind of super-optimum solution may make a lot more sense for dealing with the China population problem. It could provide small families and reproductive freedom simultaneously. Doing so requires looking to the causes of having additional children and then trying to remove or lessen those causes. One cause is a need to have children who will support parents in their old age. Adopting a more effective social security system helps eliminate or lessen that cause.

Another cause is having additional children as backup because the death rate is so high among rural Chinese children prior to age 5. Various forms of pediatric public health can make a big difference such as giving shots and using effective remedies to prevent life-jeopardizing infant diarrhea and dehydration.

A third cause is the widespread feeling that female children are worthless in terms of bringing honor to the family. One therefore keeps trying until at least one son is born. That cause can be substantially lessened by the new moves in China toward much greater opportunities for females to become lawyers, doctors, and enter other prestigious occupations. In China, women's liberation has facilitated birth control, whereas in the United States birth control has done more to facilitate women's liberation.

VII. Improving Developmental Policy

The Policy Studies Organization is embarking on an expanded program of professional developments directed toward applying policy studies to the problems of developing nations.

There are four key PSO activities in that regard, which are in the process of seeking further funding and especially participation by interested PSO members. They include:

1. A research annual on policy studies and developing nations published by JAI Press. It will contain the best long papers of the previous year or so. Further details are given in *PSJ*, Volume 17, Issue 4, at page 1002.
2. The establishment of a JAI Press multi-volume treatise on policy studies and developing nations. Further details are given in *PSJ*, Volume 17, Issue 4, at page 1003 and *PSR*, Volume 9, Issue 2, at page 433.
3. The coordination of a set of volunteer instructors to teach short courses in policy analysis skills in developing nations and eastern Europe, as part of a Peace Corps program. Further details are given in *PSR*, Volume 9, Issue 2, at pages 426 and 427.
4. The establishment of a new journal on *Policy Studies and Developing Nations*.

As part of the expansion of the Policy Studies Organization into policy studies and developing nations, the secretary-treasurer and publications coordinator has been asked by the USIA, the Asia Foundation, the Ford Foundation, and others to go to various developing nations partly to determine opportunities for PSO members and to discuss having PSO associations in those nations. The material that follows represents a summary of various ideas for improving developmental policy.

A. Pre-1989 Ideas, Especially Africa

The initial suggestions were stimulated as a result of speaking in Kenya, Malawi, Zambia, Brazil, Panama, Okinawa, and other places over the last few years. Especially helpful were conversations with leaders of the legal profession in various developing countries (such as the Malawi and Zambia Law Associations) and also leading public administrators (partly by way of the International Association for Schools and Institutes of Administration). Relevant places also include underdeveloped regions of developed countries such as the Delta region of Mississippi, the Negev Desert of Israel, and rural areas of western European countries.

The initial ideas are:

1. More help to developing countries on how to make better use of *mass labor*. This is the main resource which most developing countries have. Perhaps studies could be made of how China has used mass labor to build roads, schools, and other projects with relatively little mechanical equipment and relying heavily on local raw materials. The projects created have much more value than the workers have been paid, although the workers receive a living wage. The surplus value can then be used as a form of savings for capital investment.

2. More use of *soybeans* in developing countries to provide needed protein at relatively low cost in comparison to alternative sources of protein. Soybeans can also be converted to a variety of desired synthetic food products such as hamburgers, although the conversion costs still need to be reduced.

3. Better use of American *corn-growing* techniques with regard to hybrid seed corn, herbicides, pesticides, and inexpensive fertilizers. This includes plowing under rather than burning the stalks or letting them decompose into the air.

4. The use of more *cooperative farming* whereby equipment can be efficiently shared by way of machine tractor stations. The former Soviet Union has pioneered in that regard, but the machine tractor stations could be used in developing countries by farmers who own or at least sell their crops, rather than by collectivized farmers. The stations could dispense knowledge as well as equipment like American county agents.

5. Low cost, high leverage *medical care* that saves the lives of children. This includes preventive medicine and measures for polio, infant dehydration, malaria, leprosy, yellow fever, and nutritional diseases. Saving children greatly wins friends, although it needs to be accompanied by birth control to have less children to save and by job opportunities for when the children become adults.

6. Better planning for the movement from *rural areas to urban areas*. Such movement is inevitable as rural areas need less farmers due to more efficient farming. Such movement could learn from the experiences of other countries, including the U.S. Rural Rehabilitation Service.

7. More need for *electrification*, including at least one electrical outlet per village. Perhaps ideas could be learned from the U.S. Rural Electrification Administration.

8. More use of collectively-used *satellite dishes* to receive television programs that originate in other countries. Some television can be highly educational especially given the lack of books and other educational outlets.

9. More use of *synthetic fuels from agricultural products* such as gasohol, ethanol, and oil substitutes. Developing countries can learn from the experiences of Brazil and American corn farmers during the oil crisis. Synthetic fuels may cost more to make than oil on the world market, but developing countries need the foreign exchange for other things, and they have the raw agricultural materials for oil substitutes.

10. More help on techniques for crash programs to raise *literacy*, including literacy in English or other international languages. The successful experiences of other countries in that regard can be helpful, including Cuba and Israel. Literacy and other education programs are high leverage in building human capital.

11. More use of *systematic public policy analysis* in choosing among alternative public policies. Here the developing countries can learn from methods taught at public policy schools like Harvard, Princeton, Berkeley, Michigan, Minnesota, Texas, Pittsburgh, etc. They can also benefit from the more practical textbooks used in such courses.

12. More emphasis on *increasing national income* in order to reduce poverty, and less emphasis on redistribution of existing income. If a country is 90% poor and 10% rich, spreading the wealth of the 10% may result in the country being 100% poor because spreading that wealth makes so little difference and decreases investment incentives. A developed country that is 10% poor and 90% rich can wipe out poverty by spreading some of the wealth to the poor, but even a developed country would be better off seeking to increase its national income so as to raise living standards for virtually everybody.

13. More emphasis on increasing the national income through a program of active *governmental incentives*, including subsidies and tax breaks. That has worked well in Japan, South Korea, Taiwan, Hong Kong. and Singapore. It combines the ideas of supply-side economics and industrial policy.

14. In seeking to win friends and influence people, there should be more concentration on professors of *political science and law* in the universities of developing countries, since they train the future leaders of those countries. Also more concentration on reaching public administrators and lawyers since they are among the present leaders in developing countries.

15. More identification of the United States and developed countries with freedom of speech, fair procedure in criminal proceedings, and equal treatment under the law. This should include active encouragement of those *basic human rights*, since they generate respect for the law and increased national productivity in developing countries.

16. More *international coordination* by the United States and other developed countries in providing more systematic aid. This means coordination by way of such international associations as the United Nations, the specialized international organizations, the European Economic Community, and various

regional associations. The coordination should also involve more input from developing countries as to how the scarce resources of the developed countries might be put to better use.

These suggestions cut across all fields of human activity, but they have in common the role of political science, public policy, public administration, and public law. This is in contrast to the more usual emphasis on economics and engineering. For further details see such books as Edward Stockwell and Karen Laidlaw, *Third World Development. Problems and Prospects* (Nelson-Hall, 1981): John Lewis and Valeriana Kallab (eds.). *Development Strategies Reconsidered* (Transaction Books, 1986); William and Arline McCord, *Paths to Progress: Bread and Freedom in Developing Societies* (Norton, 1986); and Fred Lazin, et al. (eds.). *Developing Areas, Universities, and Public Policy* (Macmillan, 1988).

B. 1989, Especially China

The 16 points mentioned above were generated from trips to Africa, Latin America, and Asia prior to visiting China in May and June of 1989. The following points were especially stimulated by that visit:

1. Developing countries have an even greater need for *systematic policy analysis* and governmental decision-making than developed countries do. The United States could make many governmental mistakes over the next generation and still be a prosperous country. Developing countries, however, operate too close to the borderline of chaos, regarding their available resources, to be able to afford serious mistakes.

2. There is a need for *pragmatic experimentation*. All developing countries should not follow exactly the same model. They need to experiment in different parts of the country and different segments of the economy. That experimentation especially includes alternative ways of relating the government to the economy in terms of the marketplace, subsidies, tax breaks, regulation, and government ownership.

3. There is an especially strong need for putting resources into *educational development*. The introduction of new technologies are not so meaningful if the population does not have a sufficient educational level to be able to make good use of those technologies.

4. There is a need for encouraging innovative ideas relevant to more effective, efficient, and equitable development. This means encouraging a *pluralistic society* in terms of a free marketplace in ideas especially academic freedom, freedom of the press, freedom of assembly, and multiple interest groups, as well as more than one political party.

5. *Competition* can be a useful stimulus regardless whether it is competition between government-owned enterprises, private enterprises, or both. Competition

can also be a useful stimulus in encouraging useful ideas in the academic world and elsewhere.

6. There is a need for *higher goals*, rather than being content with merely surviving or doing better than last year, so long as the goals are not totally unrealistic. Partly achieving high goals may result in more accomplishment than completely achieving low goals.

7. There is a need for thinking more in terms of public policy solutions where all sides can *come out ahead*, rather than thinking in terms of tradeoffs and conflicts between classes, ethnic groups, age groups, the sexes, education levels, and other social divisions.

8. There is a need for more use of *positive incentives* like subsidies and tax breaks, but with strings attached. Those incentives should be designed to generate socially desired behavior, especially to increase national productivity. This can be contrasted to providing support for inefficient economic activities or support for those with powerful connections.

9. There is a need for more *professional training* in political science, public administration and public policy analysis, as contrasted to governmental decision making that is based on ideological considerations and personal connections.

10. There is a need for more participation by developing countries in international associations and other forms of *international interaction* so as to stimulate learning from each other.

11. The United States needs to play a stronger role in the use of its subsidies, tax breaks, and incentives to *encourage other countries* to adopt systems that are more pluralistic and less authoritarian and that are more pragmatic and less ideological.

12. Members of the Policy Studies Organization and others who have knowledge about policy evaluation methods should seek to share their ideas with scholars and governmental people from developing countries in *mutually beneficial interactions*.

For further details on some of the above ideas, see S. Nagel, *Higher Goals for America: Doing Better than the Best* (University Press of America, 1989). This book could have just as easily been called "Higher Goals for China" or more broadly "Higher Goals for Public Policy." The specific and cross-cutting policy problems that it deals with are virtually universal. For a more global interaction perspective, see Marvin Soroos, *Beyond Sovereignty: The Challenge of Global Policy* (University of South Carolina Press, 1986) and S. Nagel (ed.), *Global Policy Studies* (PSO-Macmillan, 1990). A journal variation on that PSO symposium is presented in the summer 1990 issue of the *International Political Science Review*. Also see M. Mills and S. Nagel (eds.), *Public Policy, Public Administration, and the People's Republic of China* (PSO-Macmillan, 1991).

C. 1990, Especially the Philippines

The interactions in Africa and Latin America resulted in an emphasis on the need for various aspects of technological development. The experiences in China resulted in an emphasis on the need for more appropriate political institutions. While in China and especially in the Philippines afterward, the emphasis partly shifted to a need to think more in terms of arriving at super-optimum solutions to public policy problems. Such solutions enable liberals, conservatives, and other major viewpoints to all come ahead of their best initial expectations simultaneously.

That kind of analysis was especially applied to five different policy problems in the Philippines. They included the minimum wage problem, commuting to and from Manila, land reform, tri-lingualism in Philippine education, and the American military bases. The minimum wage problem can be used as an illustrative example. Conservatives in the Philippines want to preserve the minimum wage at about 90 pesos a day. Liberals want it raised to 100 pesos a day. The compromise would be 95 pesos a day. The super-optimum solution might be for workers to receive 101 pesos a day, but for employers to only have to pay 89 pesos a day. The government pays the 12 pesos difference on behalf of all employers who hire workers who otherwise would be unemployed. In return for that wage supplement, the employer must agree to provide on-the-job training to upgrade the worker's skills so they are worth more than 100 pesos a day. Each worker must also agree to take and pass the training program.

VIII. NOTES

For recent general references on the concepts, methods, and examples of win-win analysis, see:

1. William Baulmol, Superfairness: Applications and Theory (MIT Press, 1986).
2. Stuart Nagel, Super-Optimum Solutions and Win-Win Policy: Basic Concepts and Methods (Greenwood, 1997).
3. Richard Noyes, Now the Synthesis: Capitalism, Socialism, and the New Social Contract (Centre for Incentive Taxation, 1991).
4. Lawrence Susskind and Jeffrey Cruikshank, Breaking the Impasse: Consensual Approaches to Resolving Public Disputes (Basic Books, 1987).
5. Stuart Nagel, Public Policy Evaluation: Making Super-Optimum Decisions (Ashgate, 1998).

For recent general references to policy studies, see:

1. Current Issues (Close Up Foundation, 1997).
2. Clarke Cochran and others, American Public Policy: An Introduction (St. Martin's, 1996).

3. William Dunn and Rita Mae Kelly, Advances in Policy Studies Since 1950 (Transaction, 1992).
4. John Hird, Controversies in American Public Policy (St. Martin's, 1995).
5. Stuart Nagel and Miriam Mills, Professional Developments in Policy Studies (Greenwood, 1993).
6. Stuart Nagel, Encyclopedia of Policy Studies (Marcel Dekker, 1994).

For further details on super-optimum policy analysis see S. Nagel, "Super-Optimum Analysis and Philippine Policy Problems," Philippine Journal of Public Administration (1990), and S. Nagel, Developing Nations and Super-Optimum Policy Analysis (PSO-Nelson-Hall, 1991). That book is one of the first in a new Policy Studies Organization Series with Nelson-Hall. That publisher is especially interested in policy analysis applied to developing nations, although so are the acquisition editors for the PSO-Macmillan and the PSO-Greenwood Series.

Thanks for stimulating the writing of the above chapter are due to Dennis Palumbo in his role as Coeditor-in-Chief of the Policy Studies Review. Thanks are also due to the USIA for funding the Africa trip, the Asia Foundation for the China trip, and the Ford Foundation for the Philippines. Thanks are especially due to the many people in those places who provided information and insights and to the many PSO people who in the future are likely to be participating in the PSO activities that relate to developing nations.

Chapter 2

ECONOMIC POLICY CONTROVERSIES

I. FOOD PRICES IN AFRICA

A. An SOS Spreadsheet Perspective

High farm prices is the conservative alternative in this context and low prices is the liberal alternative. The liberal weights involve a 3 for urban desires, a 1 for rural desires, and a 2 for all the other goals. With the liberal weights, the SOS wins 76 to 48 for all the other alternatives. We then go back and put in the conservative weights. The conservative weights give a 2 to all the neutral goals just as liberal weights do, but they do a flip-flop in urban and rural desires. For the conservative in the context, rural desires get a 3 rather than a 1, and urban desires get a 1 rather than a 3. The SOS is a winner even with the conservative weights, although now the high prices do better than they did before, but still not as well as the SOS. See Table 2.1 entitled "Pricing Food in Africa and Elsewhere."

The neutral perspective is not to give everything a weight of 1, but rather a weight of 2. If the neutrals gave everything a weight of 1, they would be giving neutral goals less weight than either the liberals or the conservatives give them. Thus the neutral picture is rural desires get a weight of 2, and so do urban desires. To the neutral, everything gets a weight of 2. The SOS wins with the neutral weights too. It is super-optimum, because it is out in front over both the conservative and liberal alternatives using both the conservative and liberal weights. It also wins over the compromise. The SOS involves the farmers getting better than high prices and the urbanites paying lower than low prices, with the government providing a supplement like the minimum wage supplement, provided that administrative feasibility is satisfied.

Administrative feasibility involves the use of food stamps. They are given to urban food buyers. They cannot be easily counterfeited. Food buyers give them to retailers, who in turn give them to wholesalers, who in turn give them to farmers, who turn them in for reimbursement. Criterion 8 just talks about political feasibility. There should be a separate criterion for administrative feasibility.

TABLE 2.1 PRICING FOOD IN AFRICA AND ELSEWHERE

CRITERIA	C Goal	L Goal	N Goal	N Goal	N Goal	N Goal	N Goal	N Goal	N Total	L Total	C Total
ALTERNATIVES	Rural Well Being	Urban Well Being	Admin. Feasibility	+ Farming Methods	+ Export	Import Technology	+ GNP	Political Feasibility	Neutral weights	Liberal weights	Conserv. weights
C Alternative											
High Price	5	1	3	4	4	4	4	1	52 (18)	48 (14)	56* (22)
L Alternative											
Low Price	1	5	3	2	2	2	2	5	44 (18)	48* (22)	40 (14)
N Alternative											
Compromise	3	3	3	3	3	3	3	3	48 (18)	48 (18)	48 (18)
S Alternative											
Price Supplement	5.1	5.1	3	5	5	5	5	5	76.4 (26.4)	76.4** (26.4)	76.4** (26.4)

NOTES:

1. The intermediate totals in parentheses are based on the first three goals. The bottom line totals are based on all the goals, including the indirect effects of the alternatives.

2. The SOS of a price supplement involves farmers receiving 101% of the price they are asking, but urban workers and other paying only 79% which is less than the 80% that they are willing and able to pay.

3. The difference of 22% is made up by food stamps given to the urban workers in return for agreeing to be in programs that upgrade their skills and productivity. The food stamps are used to pay for staple products (like rice or wheat) along with cash. Farmers can then redeem the stamps for cash, provided that they also agree to be in programs that increase their productivity.

4. Food stamps have administrative feasibility for ease in determining that workers and farmers are doing what they are supposed to do in return for the food stamps. They cannot be easily counterfeited. They serve as a check on how much the farmers have sold.

5. By increasing the productivity of farmers and workers, the secondary effects occur of improving farming methods, increasing exports, increasing the importing of new technologies, and increasing the GNP.

6. High prices are not politically feasible because of too much opposition from workers who consume, but do not produce food. The high prices though are acceptable if they can be met by way of price supplements in the form of food stamps.

Of special importance is that no farmer gets the supplement unless they agree to adopt more modern farming methods. Otherwise it is just a handout for subsidizing inefficient farming. By adopting more modern farming methods, productivity goes up. Food becomes available for export. Foreign exchange then gets acquired for importing new technology. The new technology increases the GNP, and everybody is better off, including the taxpayers who pay the supplement. They are better off because with the increased GNP, the government could even reduce taxes if it wanted to do so. It could reduce taxes below a 20% level and still have more tax revenue if the GNP base has increased substantially. Also see Table 2.2 "Simplified Table on Food Pricing."

On the broader implications of the examples, food pricing illustrates the third party benefactor which can be a very useful SOS perspective for resolving conflicts between ethnic groups, economic classes, labor versus management, landlord versus tenants.

Other examples include:

1. The landlord-tenant resolution with regard to rent vouchers.
2. The labor-management resolution with regard to the minimum wage.
3. The present example is rural versus urban and also seller versus consumers.
4. On the international front, the third party benefactor can be illustrated by the Camp David Accords.

B. An Economics Perspective[*]

Table 2.2 Simplified Table On Pricing Food

GOALS / ALTERNATIVES	C Rural well being	L Urban well being
C High price	+	-
L Low price	-	+
N Compromise	0	0
SOS OR WIN-WIN Price supplement	++	++

---

[*] This portion of the China food-prices problem is authored by Tong Daochi of the People's University of China. He also inspired the basic idea of applying super-optimizing to the food-pricing problem.

The food price has long been a big problem in China. Since the foundation of the People's Republic of China, the government, as influenced by the Soviet economic model, had adopted the policy of extremely low price of agricultural products, and high price of industrial products. That means there was a big gap between the price of industrial products and that of agricultural products. The farmers paid high "tax rate" through the form of low selling price. For this reason the farmers got little profit from agricultural production, which in return meant the farmers had not enough financial input in farming. This led to the shortage of agricultural products, as shown in Table 2.3 "An Economic Perspective on the Food Pricing SOS."

At the low price of p_0, farmers were only willing to produce and sell agricultural products at the quantity of q_0. If the price were settled by market, the equilibrium quantity would be q_1, the price would be p_1, and Δq, which is the gap between q_0, and q_1, is the shortage.

The urban people want from agriculture an abundance of farm food products at reasonable low cost, while the farmers wish to sell their products at possible high price. This is the conflict met by the government in the agricultural policy-making process, the solution to which can be used as an example of a super-optimum one.

We give the grains price as an example. The producers wish to sell at the price of 50 fen per kilogram ($1 = 3.78 yuan = 378 fen), while the highest price acceptable to the consumers is 30 fen per kilogram, as Table 2.3 shows.

The line C'C indicates that along with the decreasing of the grains price, it will cost the consumers fewer to buy the grains. That is to say, the consumers' benefit will increase. The line OF illustrates that the higher the price of the grains the farmers sell, the more benefit they will get from it, and vice versa. If the price at which the farmers sell their products is 50 fen per kilogram, and the price at which consumers buy is 30 fen per kilogram, both of the two sides can get the benefit of B_0, The compromise price would be 40 fen per kilogram, at which the consumers or the farmers might get the benefit of B_1. It might be a loss for both consumers and farmers. (As Table 2.3 indicates, $B_1 > B_0$.) It is a loss to farmers if the 50 fen per kilogram is the minimum price for them to cover the cost of the production. The 40 fen per kilogram is a loss to consumers if the 30 fen per kilogram is the maximum price that they can afford to pay at their present wages.

A super-optimum solution to this problem might involve the price at which the farmers sell their products being raised to 60 fen per kilogram, but simultaneously requiring consumers to pay only 20 fen per kilogram. The 40 fen difference would be paid by the government through the food price subsidies. Government collectively buys the agricultural products from farmers at the price of 60 fen per kilogram, then sells them to urban people at the price of 20 fen per kilogram.

At this situation, as Table 2.3 shows above, the benefit that the consumers or the farmers might get increases from B_1 to B_2 and B_2 is higher than B_0 which indicates that through the government subsidies, both the consumers and farmers can get higher benefit than their best expectation.

TABLE 2.3 AN ECONOMICS PERSPECTIVE ON THE FOOD PRICING SOS

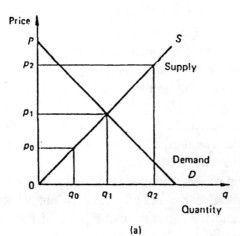

(a)

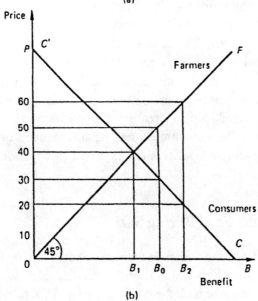

(b)

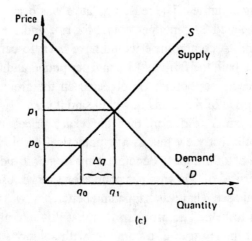

(c)

But what can the third party benefactor, the government, get from this program? It seems that the subsidies will increase the government expenditure and deficit, but what is true is that the government might especially come out ahead. This is so by virtue of the following : The increase of the supply of agricultural products. This is shown in Figure 3. If the new price P_2 is higher than the original price P_0 and the equilibrium price P_1, the supply of the agricultural products will increase from q_0 to q_2. This not only will resolve the shortage problem, but may also make the country become a food exporter. The increase of input to the land by farmers. This in return will reduce the government investment on agriculture. The decrease of the inflation rate. This is very important for the economic reform and development of China.

In fact, the beginning of the economic reform of China was in the rural area in the later 1970's, with the adoption of the Family-Contract-Responsibility-System in agricultural production and the increase of the price of the agricultural products that government bought from farmers. From 1980-1984 the quantity of the crops production reached the highest point in Chinese history. But since 1985, the agricultural economic growth has been stagnated. The reasons might involve many aspects, but one of the important factors leading rural economy to this situation is the increase of the price of the industrial products that are used in farming, such as farm machinery, seeds, fuels, and pesticides. The benefit that farmers got from the rising of the price of agricultural products has been covered by the increase in the cost of the agribusiness input. In order to change this situation, the government has made the decision of increasing input on agriculture. New agricultural policies are expected to be made and implemented in the 1990's.

C. A Reaction to the Food Pricing SOS

A social scientist from a prominent international organization came up after the above presentation in Morocco. He said he could not accept the idea of a food supplement that would make both the rural farmers and the urban workers simultaneously better off in developing countries. The reason he gave was because the example said that the farmers in China wanted 20 cents per pound for rice and the workers wanted to pay only 10 cents per pound. A compromise would have been 15 cents per pound. The food supplement would have paid the farmers 21 cents per pound and the workers would have had to pay only nine cents per pound. He objected on the grounds that he had recently been to China and the price of rice was not what I said it was.

The chair of the panel told him that the exact prices might be an irrelevant consideration. He should just view this as a hypothetical problem to see the big picture with regard to the idea of a third party benefactor making both sides come out better. The chair suggested that instead of 20 cents per pound for rice he just use algebraic symbols and that maybe he would see what was happening better.

That did not seem to help. The problem was that this international organization has spent large amounts of money trying to come up with solutions for exactly this kind of problem. His mind apparently was so narrowly focused that he refused to recognize any kind of solution that he had not thought of or that other people at his institution had not thought of. Therefore he clutched for whatever straw he could find to argue that this was not a solution.

The moral of the story is not to provide any straws. One has to be careful about the details, even if the details are irrelevant. For instance, the correct figure is $200 per week (instead of $800 per month) for the subscription fulfillment and related costs of the Policy Studies Organization. Which figure one uses makes no difference at all in comparing a set of alternative proposals. Nevertheless, someone like this international executive will say we cannot accept this analysis because the correct figure is really $200 per week and not $800 per month. Just like the correct figure for a pound of rice in China as of July 20, 1989 when the presentation was made was actually about 12 cents per pound. I said it was somewhere between 10 and 20 cents, implying that it was 15 cents. If an intelligent international executive could say that destroys the whole idea of super-optimum solutions, then less intelligent, less knowledgeable people might be even more likely to find a defense mechanism. Such a mechanism enables them to avoid explicitly or indirectly admitting that they might have been scooped on a solution. It also avoids allowing the opposition side to come out ahead regardless how well one's own side comes out ahead.

II. Africa Small Business Problem

The business development problem is very time-oriented in that it talks about small businesses as a stepping stone over time to big businesses. The shortsighted people say we have unemployment, especially unemployed women. We must give them something to do and give them dead-end jobs making clothes and selling clothes, or even worse, growing fruits and vegetables and selling those.

The people with more of a time horizon say, the big problem is not eating a fish for today but learning how to fish or doing some kind of activity that has some payoff beyond today or this week. In that context it may involve sending the women to school to learn how to be computer operators. The business development context as contrasted to the education and skills upgrading context is let's start them out in a small machine shop where they make spark plugs. You cannot make spark plugs as fast as you can make dishcloths or as fast as you can go into the countryside and pick wild rhubarb to sell. To make spark plugs you have to first of all get the machines to make them with and you have to learn to operate the machines. Maybe no income will come in for a couple of months, whereas income can be immediate in selling sweaters or casaba plants. In a few months, spark plugs are being made and sold, maybe with more income although more expense than selling fruits and vegetables so that even at first it is less profitable. The key thing though is that it can lead to becoming a factory. It can lead to the manufacturing of spark plugs on larger scale or can lead to manufacturing of other auto parts. That in turn leads to the employment of more people including both men and women. It may even lead to producing more spark plugs than the local economy can buy because the local economy does not have many cars or trucks. That could mean exporting the surplus spark plugs to places that supply foreign money, hard currency for buying bigger machines for making maybe bumpers, fenders, windshield wipers, and maybe even cars eventually but not necessarily. Making cars in developing nations is frequently not productive; it is just a status symbol activity. Cars can be made better in Japan or even in the United States. That's getting into something very complex that involves lots of components coming from different places. A spark plug may be nothing but some porcelain and some metal and one machine that makes the whole spark plug. There is no such thing as a machine that makes a whole car.

The super-optimum solution is deliberately choosing small businesses that have a high or relatively speaking higher capability of becoming big businesses even though it takes a while for even the small business form to pay off. See Table 2.4 "Business Development and Africa." That is part of long-term thinking. It is the idea of delayed gratification and also of taking one step back in order to take two steps forward later. It is a way of thinking that has not been so present in equatorial countries where there is a tradition that if you want to eat, you do not have to do a lot of planting in the springtime and wait all the way until autumn to harvest something to eat. Instead, you just go out and shake a coconut tree and you have food. That works fine for coconuts. It does not work so fine for pharmaceuticals. There is no pharmaceutical tree, although there is to some extent in that developing nations do sometimes make good use of herbs. For sure there is no automobile tree.

Table 2.4. Business Development And Africa

GOALS / ALTERNATIVES	C Easy feasibility	L Value to economy
C Large business	+	—
L Small business	—	+
N Medium business	0	0
SOS OR WIN-WIN Small to large (especially manufacturing)	++	++

Nobody worried about automobiles 100 years ago because they did not exist 100 years ago. Africa was blessed with being on the equator and having no need for heavy clothes, heavy houses, or heavy agriculture. The climate was warm all year round and wild food was plentiful. That has partly become a bit of a curse in the sense of creating limited time horizons with regard to delaying gratification. The concern of the Africa Development Bank for long-term development is well-placed. Africa is less concerned with long-term development than any other of the four regions, partly because it has more land mass and more people along the equator than Asia does or Latin America, and certainly a lot more than East Europe, which is a long way from the equator. East Europe may be almost in the opposite problem where it is so cold that people are paralyzed from doing things because it is too cold to do much of anything. At the equator people are paralyzed from doing anything because in the past there has been so little need to do things.

One thing to strongly emphasize is that this is not climatic determinism, because human beings are quite capable of overcoming whatever climate they happen to live in. Climate might shape things in prehistoric times, but modern people can live luxuriously in Antarctica if they want to do so, or on the equator in central Africa. We have refrigerators for central Africa and we have effective heating devices for the Antarctic. It is a matter of to a considerable extent public policy stimulating the use of appropriate technology.

The words appropriate technology is sometimes used by the backpackers to mean virtually no technology at all. It should be used to mean that what is good technology for the Antarctic may not be good technology for central Africa but that humans have developed technologies that can deal with any climates or any kind of geographical factors. People could live luxuriously at the top of the Himalaya Mountains or well below sea level as long as they are not under water. If necessary, we could even live under water and pump oxygen in, but that is rather unnecessary.

III. THE ASIAN LABOR SHORTAGE

A. The Problem

Speaking before the Hong Kong government, they in effect said that they did not especially want to hear about solar energy versus nuclear energy, or trials versus pleas, or getting married, or any of those other examples (although we never got to presenting any of them anyhow). They wanted to know about an SOS to a problem involving Hong Kong that they considered to be a crucial problem that they were not able to work out.

The labor shortage was such a problem, which they were approaching from a very traditional perspective. On one hand was to import additional labor. It required no importing at all. All it required doing was to just stop arresting people who are seeking to cross the borders from every direction. These include the Vietnamese boat people, the people from the Chinese mainland, the Filipinos, and even some people from English speaking places (although not many) like Australia, Britain, or India. Most English speaking people are a little cautious about settling or staying in Hong Kong given that it will become a Chinese province in 1997.

It thus creates a dilemma that paralyzes decision-making if the choice is one of retaining the labor shortage and thereby missing out on opportunities to make Hong Kong even more prosperous than it is versus allowing labor in and thereby diluting the population of Hong Kong. This is partly a racist thing but is also a legitimate concern for a lot of expense involved in education and welfare, although the immigrants may be especially ambitious people who in the long run will pay more than their share of taxes. This may be especially true of the Vietnamese boat people, although coming by boat from Vietnam to Hong Kong is not much more difficult than crossing the border from Mexico to Texas. They are, however, giving up whatever they had in Vietnam.

The SOS that seemed to be a kind of blind spot by virtue of how the terms were defined is simply to redefine the labor force, and then they suddenly have a labor surplus. Redefining the labor force means recognizing all the potential labor they have by virtue of elderly people who are capable of working who are not doing so, disabled people, mothers of preschool children, people with part-time or seasonal jobs, people who are looking for second jobs, and especially people whose jobs and productivity could be upgraded. See Table 2.5 "Asian Labor Shortage."

B. The SOS Table for Conservatives and Liberals

The alternatives are:

(C1)   Import cheap labor.
(C2)   Preserve national purity.
(L1)   Preserve union wages.
(L2)   Provide immigrant opportunities.
(N)   Import some labor but less than either C1 or L2 would like but more than C2 or L1 would like.
(SOS) Add to the labor force and increase labor productivity. That sounds a bit ambiguous since one can add to the labor force by importing labor. In this context it means adding by drawing upon people who are already part of the society.

One key *goal* would be to increase the GNP, especially by filling orders that otherwise would not be filled. A second key goal is to minimize disruption to the existing society. It looks as if a general pattern tends to be emerging in developing these tables of having one relatively liberal goal and one relatively conservative goal with other goals being relatively less important or unimportant.

The *scoring* tends to involve the conservative alternative doing mildly negative on the liberal goal and mildly positive on the conservative goal, and the opposite with the liberal alternative. The neutral alternative does in the middle on both goals and the-SOS alternative does especially well on both goals. Table 2.5 shows six alternatives, two goals, and twelve scores, as well as totals reflecting weights for nativism, unionism, and an open door policy.

TABLE 2.5 THE ASIAN LABOR SHORTAGE

CRITERIA ALTERNATIVES	C_1L_2 Goal +GNP	C_2L_1 Goal -Disruption to Society	N Total Neutral weights	Total L_1 & C_2 Weights Nativism & Unionism	Total L_2 & C_1 Weights Open Door Policy
C_1 Alternative Import Cheap Labor	4	2	12	10	14*
C_2 Alternative Preserve National Purity	2	4	12	14*	10
L_1 Alternative Preserve Union Wages	2	4	12	14*	10
L_2 Alternative Provide Immigrant Opportunities	4	2	12	10	14*
N Alternative Import Some Labor	3	3	12	12	12
S Alternative +Labor Force +Productivity	5	5	20	20**	20**

In this example there are two conservative alternatives and two liberal alternatives. It is not appropriate to say that one conservative alternative is more conservative than another, and that one liberal alternative is more liberal than another. They are just two different kinds of conservatism, and two different kinds of liberalism. One kind of conservatism is basically pro-business and is interested in maximizing business profits. The other kind of conservatism is basically nationalist bordering on racist and is more concerned with ethnic purity than it is with profits. One type of liberalism is pro-union. It is concerned with union wages. It is pocketbook liberalism. It is not concerned with civil liberties. The other liberalism focuses more on civil liberties. For labels we could say that we are talking about business conservatives versus cultural conservatives, and hard-hat liberals versus civil libertarian liberals. Those are reasonably neutral terms as contrasted to more derogatory or laudatory terms like mercenary conservatives versus racist conservatives, and pocketbook liberals versus intellectual liberals. Intellectual liberals sounds laudatory. Spiro Agnew called them effete, egghead, or pinhead liberals, which does not sound so laudatory.

There are other kinds of conservatives and liberals, but they are not all involved on the immigration issue. There are also religious conservatives who are very strong on issues that have to do with abortion, pornography, or prayer in the schools who are not necessarily pro-business or racist, although there may be overlap. Likewise, one can talk about a set of liberals who are particularly concerned with doing things for poor people. The hard-hat unionists are not very sympathetic to people on welfare. The civil libertarians may be concerned with the free speech rights and due process rights of people on welfare, but not necessarily advocates of bigger handouts. They may even be advocates of placing all kinds of strings on handouts, which would go contrary to the welfare liberals, just as the idea of strings goes contrary to the laissez-faire conservatives. At the present time, one can talk about two kinds of pro-business conservatives, those who want to do things for business but with strings attached, and those who want to do things for business but with no strings attached. Likewise, the liberals can be classified into those who want to do things for poor people with no strings attached, versus those who recognize that strings may be good for poor people and society.

In terms of the *initial totals*, some recognizable patterns are also emerging. All the alternatives tend to wind up with total scores of 12 except the SOS alternative, because they all tend to do mildly well for a 4 on one goal and mildly poorly for a 2 on the second goal, or a 3 on both.

The liberal totals in this context favor alternatives C1 and L2. That depends on what kind of liberal we are talking about, though. Maybe we have to say that both goals are ambivalent goals. An increased GNP is normally a liberal goal, but would be opposed by unionists in this context if it means importing cheap competitive labor in order to achieve it. Therefore it would only be a liberal goal in the eyes of the L2 liberals. It is also a conservative goal in the eyes of the C1 conservatives. This could be a good example of where it is not meaningful to refer to the goals as being conservative or liberal.

Each goal is supported by both liberals and conservatives intensely, but different kinds of liberals and conservatives. In the usual situation all goals are supported by liberals and by conservatives, but the liberals like some goals relatively better than the conservatives do, and vice versa. Here it is not that the liberals like some goals relatively better than the conservatives do. It is that some liberals like some of the goals better than other liberals do. Likewise, some conservatives like some of the goals better than other conservatives do. In other words, there is a kind of conflict within conservatives on the goals as well as on the alternatives, and it might thus be meaningless to talk about a liberal total and a conservative total. One could talk about an L1 liberal total and an L2 liberal total and a C1 conservative total and a C2 conservative total. In that regard, increasing the GNP is a C1 goal and an L2 goal. Decreasing societal disruption is a C2 and an L1 goal.

That complicates the assigning of weights a bit, but not that much. Table 2.5 shows how each group would weight the goals. Knowing that, we can calculate in our heads what the totals should look like. The subtotals could be put on the table. There are only two multipliers, namely 3 and 1. It is easy enough to show what each relation score becomes when multiplied by 3 and when multiplied by 1. We do not have to write anything down to show what each raw score becomes when multiplied by 1.

Calculating the four sets of new totals:

1. For the L1 or unionist set, the winner is either preserve national purity or preserve union wages. They both amount to the same thing in terms of whether external labor should be excluded or imported. One could say that there are strange bedfellows between the racist conservatives and exclusionary unionists. Nothing very strange about that at all. It has occurred at many times in American history where otherwise economic-liberal union members would take sexist or racist positions.

2. The L2 or civil libertarian column has intellectuals and business people joining together because they share a willingness to allow for more open immigration, even though their reasons may be different.

3. On the C1 or business column the results turn out to be the same as the L2 column because in the context of this subject matter and these goals, the business people who want to import cheap labor come out with the same totals as the intellectuals who want to provide more immigrant opportunities. We can get differences in those columns if we were to add a goal like "increase individual firm profits" which would please the business types, but not necessarily the intellectual types. If we added a goal called "reward ambitious immigrants," that would please the intellectual types, but not necessarily the business types. We would have to add two goals like that in order to get a difference between the L2 column and the C1 column. We would then have to add 2 more goals to get a difference between the L1 and the C2 column.

4. The C2 or nativist column which reflects the goals of those who want to preserve national purity comes out the same as the L1 column, which reflects the goals of those who want to preserve union wages.

We could force C2 and L1 to be separate in the United States by adding a goal like "encourage white Anglo-Saxon Protestantism." That might please those who want to preserve national purity, but it would not please the average unionist who tends to be Polish, Italian, Irish, Hispanic, or otherwise Catholic. Likewise, we could add a goal that would please the unionists, but not please the ethnic purity people. All we have to do is just add a goal that is the opposite of encouraging white Anglo-Saxon Protestantism, such as encouraging diversity of religion and language in the United States. That is the opposite of preserving national purity, but it would be likely to please most unionists since they tend to be minority group people, at least in terms of religion if not race.

All that can be said verbally without cluttering up the table by adding four more goals. As of now the table has seven columns. That would give it 11 columns which is not so horrendous, although the standard table only allows for nine. A main reason for not adding those goals is not because they would make the table too complicated, but because they are not as relevant to the immigration issue as the goals that we currently have. We could add just two more columns, since there is no reason why we have to add one column that talks in terms of promoting a single ethnic group (versus pluralism), and then another column that talks in terms of doing the opposite.

The best way to handle the problem is to just note that although the L1 and C2 groups come out with the same bottom line and also the L2 and C1 groups, they do so for different reasons. This table is not designed to explicitly indicate what those different reasons are. It is just designed to bring out which alternative is the best in light of the alternatives available and the goals to be achieved. The verbalization can discuss the motives behind why different groups may place the same high value or low value on a goal for different reasons. It can also say why two groups have the same reasons but yet they are different groups because they differ with regard to other matters. Also see Table 2.6 "Simplified Table on Asian Labor Shortage."

C. The SOS Alternative

Instead of concentrating on the diversity within conservatives and liberals, we could put more emphasis on the idea of solving the problem by raising goals above what is considered the best. That means raising the unemployment goal to be higher than just achieving zero percent unemployment in the traditional sense. That sense does not count large segments of the population as being unemployed. It simply defines them out of the labor force. It also does not count large segments of the labor force as being under-employed. Instead it defines being employed as simply having a job, regardless how part-time or how beneath one's capabilities.

Doing better than what was formerly considered the best is now only one kind of SOS. It may be less interesting in at least some ways, because it may be simply a matter of definition, not a matter of actively pursuing well-placed subsidies, tax breaks, or new policies. One, however, does not solve the labor shortage problem simply by defining elderly people as being unemployed. One has to go further and talk about how to provide them with employment opportunities. We may, however, make a big difference if we start calling so-called retired people unemployed. Just calling them unemployed may stimulate them to become more interested in finding jobs, and it could stimulate potential employers into doing more to seek them out. The concept of being retired creates an image of somebody who is practically dead, senile, or decrepit in some sense. On the other hand, the concept of unemployed (especially temporarily unemployed) creates an image of an able-bodied person who is willing and able to work if provided with appropriate opportunities.

Table 2.6 Simplified Table on Asian Labor Shortage

GOALS / ALTERNATIVES	C Increase GNP	L Decrease disruption to society
C		
1. Import cheap labor		
2. Preserve national purity	+	-
L		
1. Preserve union wages		
2. Provide immigrant opportunities	-	+
N		
1. Import some labor	0	0
SOS OR WIN-WIN		
1. Increase labor force		
2. Increase productivity	++	++

In all the examples of doing better than the best by redefining best, we are talking about more than just definitions. How things are labeled does influence the behavior of the people who are so labeled, or the doers of the activities. It also influences the behavior and attitudes of other people toward those activities. In the Hong Kong labor context, the super-optimum alternative involves the means for achieving the super-optimum goal of doing better than zero percent unemployment. All the other alternatives focus on the tradeoff between importing labor and disrupting society, or not importing labor and losing additional prosperity.

D. Broader Implications

The Hong Kong labor problem illustrates labor problems throughout the world, not just Hong Kong. Every country either has a labor shortage or a labor surplus. Virtually no country considers its labor situation to be exactly in balance regarding supply and demand. The countries with a shortage are more dramatic like Japan, Korea, Taiwan, Singapore, Hong Kong, Malaysia, West Germany, and to some extent the United States. The countries with a labor surplus consist of most of the underdeveloped countries that are willing to export labor. That includes all of Central America that exports labor to the U.S. and northern South America that does some exporting to Argentina and Chile, but not much except in the sense of unskilled labor. Although that is primarily the kind of labor that is exported. The big exporting to the U.S. is, however, at both ends, unskilled labor from Mexico but a skilled brain drain from throughout the world, including China,

India, eastern Europe, and western Europe. South Africa to a considerable extent operates as a labor importer from the front-line states, but strictly unskilled labor. It loses skilled labor to the rest of the world, including the U.S. and Canada. Israel is another example. They import lots of unskilled labor from the West Bank but lose their skilled labor at the top to the U.S. The Hong Kong problem is primarily one of the need for more labor at the bottom. It is not the kind of unskilled labor that works in the mines of South Africa, but instead the semi-skilled labor that works in the assembly plants throughout Asia, or at least throughout the Asian countries that have that kind of labor shortage.

The problem illustrates the need for having international economic communities like the EEC or European Economic Community, or the more recent ASEAN which stands for Asian Economic Association of Nations. if such an international community functions properly, then the countries that have labor surpluses export to the countries that have labor shortages and everybody is better off. There could also be interchange between economic communities. There is. Not in the sense that the Philippines is exporting labor to western Europe, but in the sense that the Philippines is the largest source of labor in the Arab Middle East, and they send a lot of people to Hong Kong, China, and the U.S.

On a more methodological level, the Hong Kong labor problem illustrates better than any other problem the idea of multiple liberal groups and multiple conservative groups that do not get along with each other.

Another general principle which this example illustrates is the importance of how a policy problem is labeled. If the problem is referred to as the labor shortage problem of Hong Kong or Asia, then this tends to lead to a solution of importing more labor. If the problem is referred to as an immigration problem or an ethnic relations problem, then this tends to lead to a solution of avoiding the importing of more labor. The best way to refer to the problem is in such a way that one is pushed toward neither solution, but instead toward thinking in terms of a super-optimum solution in which all sides can come out ahead of their best expectations. That might mean referring to the problem as the under-employment problem of Hong Kong or Asia. Calling it that leads one to thinking about how to make more effective use of willing and able people who are outside of the labor force, and of people inside the labor force who are not working up to their full potential abilities.

IV. SOME COMPARISONS BETWEEN JAPANESE AND AMERICAN PRODUCTIVITY

The typical Japanese firm wants to be the most important firm in the industry even if it is losing money. The typical American firm is happy with being 20th in the industry if it is making profits.

The big indicator should be which of those 2 basic orientations is better for society and the global market. The Japanese approach is much better if becoming first in the industry is achieved by making high quality products at low prices, even if the firm almost goes bankrupt doing so. The world benefits even if the firm loses. The American firm that is making big profits and providing the world with low quality merchandise at high prices is obviously less socially desirable.

Japanese firms are sometimes killing themselves not out of altruism, but out of a desire to be on top. But not to be on top by using cheap-shot advertising with sexy girls on American cars which just appeals to people's worst instincts in getting them to buy products.

Both the American firms and the Japanese firms are operating to promote their own self-interests. The difference is that the Japanese concept of self-interest is to be acclaimed as the leader in the field. The American concept is just to make a lot of money even if the products are disliked, as long as you can sell them for more than they cost to make. American products are not necessarily disliked, but they are sometimes laughed at like gas guzzlers in developing countries.

Even on R & D, American firms do not deserve so much credit. Most American R & D is developed in American universities, not American business firms. The U.S. deserves a lot of credit for inventiveness, including the winning of Nobel prizes, but that is not GM. That is the University of Illinois and other universities. Japan does poorly on that score in both its business firms and its universities. They are not such contributors to the world when it comes to inventiveness. They are especially implementers, rather than inventors.

Each business firm in the world trying to maximize income minus expenses is by no means good for the world, rather than maximizing market share. This does more to refute Adam Smith and traditional capitalism than anything Karl Marx had to say. Marx was operating largely out of theory, rather than out of the experience that had not yet arrived in the world. The Japanese business firms are doing well in that they are moving toward 100% of the market share in many basic industries of the world. They will probably never reach the point of 100%, but that is what they are striving for. Yet they or their companies are not getting rich, in terms of income over expenses and assets over liabilities. The reasons are:

1. They charge low prices that hurt how much profit they can make on a Toyota or Sony TV set because they want to sell a lot of Toyotas. They want as a high a percent of the market as possible.

2. They provide all kinds of benefits to the consumer that are expensive to the manufacturer but that help sell their products and thereby increase their market share.

3. They thus almost deviate substantially from what is taught in American business schools. They are lowering their revenue by lowering their prices. They are increasing their expenses by offering various features that no regulatory agency is requiring them to offer.

4. Yet they are greatly disrupting the business of U.S. Steel, GM, and other giants of American industry. Japan is benefiting because it means lots of income for Japanese workers and lots of income in the form of taxes for Japanese governments. The Japanese CEO's are not exactly impoverished, but they do not

live as luxuriously as the people who run GM and U.S. Steel who are doing a poorer job.

Competition is fine for the qualify of life of the world and a nation that competes well like Japan does. That, however, is not advertising-competition. It is also not cheating competition where a business firm sees how much it can cheat its customers or cheat it workers. It is competition to see who can produce the most sought-after product because of its low price and its quality content. That may be crazy behavior, but Japan as a nation is laughing hysterically all the way to the bank.

A. Basic SOS Concepts Using Minimum Wage Policy

Table 2.7 presents the Philippine minimum wage problem in the context of an SOS framework, table, matrix, chart, spreadsheet, or other synonym for a set of rows and columns. An SOS table shows the goals to be achieved on the columns, the policy alternatives available on the rows, the relations between alternatives and goals in the cells, various overall totals for the alternatives at the far right, and a capability of determining what it would take to bring a second-place or other-place alternative up to first place.

TABLE 2.7 THE PHILIPPINE MINIMUM WAGE PROBLEM

CRITERIA ALTERNATIVES	L Goal Decent Wages	C Goal -Overpayment	N Total Neutral weights	L Total Liberal weights	C Total Conservative weights
C Alternative 90 per day	2	4	12	10	14*
L Alternative 100 per day	4	2	12	14*	10
N Alternative 95 per day	3	3	12	12	12
S Alternative 101 to worker, 89 from employer, 12 wage supplement	5	5	20	20**	20**

To be an SOS table rather than just an ordinary decision-analysis table, it is necessary that there be at least one conservative, liberal, and SOS alternative The conservative alternative can generally be considered as representing the best expectations of the conservatives, although their best expectations may be better expressed in terms of the degree of goal achievement they might best expect. The liberal alternative generally reflects the best expectations of the liberals. The SOS alternative (if it really is an SOS alternative) is capable of exceeding both the conservative and liberal best expectations in terms of their respective alternatives and/or goals.

1. The Inputs

In the context of the Philippine minimum wage problem as of January, 1990, the conservatives would like to keep the minimum wage down to about 90 pesos per day, The liberals would like to get the minimum wage up to about 100 pesos per day. The neutral alternative usually splits the difference between the conservative and liberal alternative or takes a little of each. In this context the neutral or compromise alternative is 95 pesos per day.

The goals of both the conservatives and liberals are to pay decent wages but to avoid overpayment. The important thing in this context is not determining exactly what a decent wage is, but the relativistic idea that 100 pesos scores better on achieving a decent wage than 90 pesos does. Likewise, 90 pesos scores better on avoiding overpayment than 100 pesos does.

Instead of (or in addition to) expressing those relations in words, we can summarize them by using relativistic numbers on a 1-5 scale. On such a scale, a 5 means that the alternative is highly conducive to the goal relative to the other alternatives. A 4 means mildly conducive; a 3 means neither conducive nor adverse; a 2 means mildly adverse; and a 1 means the alternative is highly adverse to the goal.

In the context of the Philippine minimum wage problem, one could give the liberal alternative a 4 on decent wages, the conservative alternative a 2, and the neutral alternative a 3. Those are just relative numbers. It would be just as meaningful to use the numbers 400, 200, and 300, or 12, 6, and 9. The important characteristic is the rank order, and to a less extent the relative distances. Rank order is especially important and also relative distance because the bottom line in policy evaluation is determining which alternative ranks first and best.

Likewise on avoiding overpayment, the conservative alternative receives a 4, the liberal alternative a 2, and the neutral alternative a 3. We are temporarily not mentioning the exact nature of the SOS alternative. We need to first clarify the analysis working with the more traditional alternatives to the minimum wage problem, or whatever the policy problem might be.

After determining the basic alternatives, goals, and relations, the next step in an SOS analysis is to discuss the relative weights of the goals. A 1-3 scale is a simple and frequent way of measuring the relative weights or importance of the goals. With such a scale, a 3 means highly important relative to the other goals. A 2 means middling important, and a 1 means having relatively low but positive importance.

In the minimum wage context, liberals tend to assign "decent wages" a relatively high weight and assign "avoiding overpayment" a relatively low weight. Thus liberals would implicitly or explicitly multiply the scores in the decent-wages column by a 3, and multiply the scores in the avoid-overpayment column by a 1. Doing so results in a liberal total score for the conservative alternative of 10, which is 3 x 2 plus 1 x 4. The liberal total for the liberal alternative is 14, which is 3 x 4 plus 1 x 2, and so on for determining the other numbers in the liberal total column.

2. The Total Scores and the SOS

The conservative total scores are calculated in a similar way. Conservatives tend to give "decent wages" a weight of 1 and "avoiding overpayment" a weight of 3. The conservative alternative thus receives a conservative total of 14, which is 1 x 2 plus 3 x 4. Neutrals tend to give all goals a middling weight of 2. Thus the conservative alternative gets a neutral total of 12, which is 2 x 2 plus 2 x 4. An easier way to calculate the neutral totals is to simply add the raw scores of 2 plus 4 to obtain 6, and then double that unweighted total.

Notice that on the liberal totals, the liberal alternative wins or ranks first before taking into consideration the SOS alternative, and the conservative alternative ranks third. Likewise on the conservative totals, the conservative alternative ranks first, and the liberal alternative scores last, before considering the SOS alternative. That is a check on internal consistency, although such consistency may not always be completely present.

Under the SOS alternative, each worker receives 101 pesos a day as a minimum wage. Each employer, however, only pays 89 pesos per day to the workers. The difference of 12 pesos comes from a governmental minimum-wage supplement. By each worker receiving more than 100 pesos, the SOS alternative has exceeded the best expectations of the liberals. By each employer paying less than 90 pesos, the SOS alternative has also exceeded the best expectations of the conservatives.

The SOS alternative receives a 5 on the goal of decent wages because it involves paying the workers even more than the liberal alternative which received a 4, assuming one wants to round off to whole numbers on the 1-5 scale, although that is not necessary. The SOS alternative also receives a 5 on the goal of avoiding overpayment because it involves employers paying even less than the conservative alternative which received a 4. Thus SOS alternative receives a total score of 20 on the neutral totals which is 10 x 2. It receives a score of 20 on the liberal totals which is 3 x 5 plus 1 x 5, and it receives a score of 20 on the conservative totals which is 1 x 5 plus 3 x 5. It is a super-optimum solution because it exceeds the best expectations of both liberals and conservatives simultaneously. Also see Table 2.8, "Simplified Table on the Philippine Minimum Wage Problem."

3. Potential Criticism

To be truly super-optimum, however, the SOS alternative should not involve liberals and conservatives both coming out ahead at the expense of other major parties or viewpoints. In this context, one might argue that the government or the general public comes out behind as a result of the extra tax-cost to provide for the minimum wage supplement. It is a subsidy to the wages of the workers, and a subsidy to the available payroll money of the employers.

A well placed subsidy is professionally administered and involves enough money to get the job done. It especially involves strings attached that make the subsidy more than worthwhile to the government and the taxpayer. In the context of a minimum wage supplement, one important string might be to require the employers to hire people who would otherwise be unemployed, and to require the workers to be willing to move to jobs where they are needed. Another important string would be to require the employers to provide on-the-job training to upgrade the skills of the workers so they will be more productive than 101 pesos per day, and to require the workers to participate in the training so they can pass whatever performance tests are involved.

Table 2.8 Simplified Table on Minimum Wage Problem

ALTERNATIVES \ GOALS	C Overpayment	L Decent wages
C 90 per day	+	-
L 100 per day	-	+
N 95 per day	0	0
SOS OR WIN-WIN 101 to worker, 89 from employer, 12 wage supplement	++	++

With those strings attached, the taxpayers would be relieved from various welfare burdens such as providing medical care, food stamps, unemployment compensation, public housing, aid to dependent children, social security, disability aid, and other forms of public aid. Providing jobs to the unemployed and upgrading job skills facilitate better role models, thereby relieving the taxpayers of the possible welfare burdens of the future generation. The new employment and increased income lessens costly anti-social behavior and attitudes, such as crime, drugs, vice, bitterness, and depression. The upgraded employment adds to the gross national product, helps create jobs for others, and adds to the tax base.

One objection might be that paying the unemployed 101 pesos per day will antagonize those who are already employed at the old minimum wage of about 95 pesos per day. That is not a serious problem in the United States because there are relatively few workers right at the minimum wage, and they tend to be non-union with little political power. In the Philippines and other developing countries, however, there is a relatively high percentage of the work force at the minimum wage, and they tend to be unionized and more aggressive. Thus, the string about on-the-job training might have to be emphasized in the Philippines more than the hiring of the unemployed, as compared to the United States.

Another objection might be that employers will resist providing the on-the-job training. They are not so likely to do so if it is being partly subsidized by the wage supplement of 12 pesos a day. They are also not so likely to object if the training is reasonably well-planned so that worker productivity increases more than the cost, thereby increasing the profits of the employers.

This is thus a potential super-optimum solution for conservative employers, liberal workers, and the total society of taxpayers. A key reason this and other super-optimum solutions are sometimes not adopted is because the policy-makers until recently have not been thinking along these lines. Another reason is that too often liberals are too concerned that conservatives might gain by a super-optimum solution, even though liberals also gain. Likewise, conservatives may be too concerned that liberals might gain, even though conservatives also gain.

One might also argue that there is something about the minimum wage situation which makes things too easy to find a super-optimum solution. The examples which follow deal with a variety of subject matters and approaches to arriving at super-optimum solutions. They include (1) bicycles versus cars in Beijing, (2) trying to commute to and from Manila, (3) food prices in China, (4) land reform in the Philippines, (5) raising faculty salaries without raising taxes in China, (6) tri-lingualism in Philippine education, (7) the Asian labor shortage, and (8) American military bases. These examples draw upon the author's 1989-90 experiences in China and the Philippines, but they could apply to any developing or developed country by reasoning from analogy.

V. PRIVATIZATION

The changes that are occurring in Eastern Europe and in many other regions and nations of the world provide an excellent opportunity to apply systematic policy analysis to determining such basic matters as how to organize the economy, the government, and other social institutions. Population control and land reform are highly important problems, but they may not be as basic as reconstituting a society.

A. Alternatives

Table 2.9 "Government versus Ownership and Operations" analyzes the fundamental issue of socialism versus capitalism in the context of government versus private ownership and operation of the basic means of producing industrial and agricultural products. The essence of socialism in this content is government ownership and operation of factories and farms or at least those larger than the handicraft or garden-size, as in the Soviet Union of 1960. The essence of capitalism is private ownership and operation of both factories and farms, as in the United States of 1960. The neutral position or middle way is to have some government and some private ownership-operation, as in Sweden of 1960. The year 1960 is used because that is approximately when the Soviet Union began to change with the advent of Nikita Khruschev. The United States also underwent big changes in the 1960s with the advent of John F. Kennedy.

Table 2.9 refers to government ownership-operation as the liberal or left-wing alternative, as it is in the United States and in world history at least since the time of Karl Marx. The table refers to private ownership-operation as the conservative or right-wing alternative, as it is in the U.S. and elsewhere at least since the time of Adam Smith. In recent years in the Soviet Union and in China, those favoring privatization have been referred to as liberals, and those favoring retention of government ownership-operation have been referred to as conservatives. The labels make no difference in this context. The object of Table 2.9 is to find a super-optimum solution that more than satisfies the goals of both ideologies or groups, regardless or their labels.

B. Goals and Relations

The key capitalistic goal is high productivity in terms of income-producing goods substantially above what it costs to produce them. The key socialistic goal is equity in terms of the sharing of ownership, operation, wealth, and income. Other goals that tend to be more socialistic than capitalistic, but are less fundamental consist of (1) workplace quality, including wages, hours, safety, hiring by merit, and worker input, (2) environmental protection, including reduction of air, water, radiation, noise, and other forms of pollution, and (3) consumer protection, including low prices and goods that are durable, safe, and high quality.

Going down the productivity column, the liberal socialistic alternative does not score so high on productivity for a lack of profit-making incentives and a surplus of bureaucratic interference in comparison to the capitalistic alternative, assuming the level of technology is held constant. The empirical validity of that statement is at least partially confirmed by noting that the capitalistic countries of Japan and West Germany are more productive than their socialistic counterparts of East Germany and China, although they began at approximately the same level as of 1945 at the end of World War II. Going down the equity column, the liberal socialistic alternative does score relatively high. By definition, it involves at least a nominal collective sharing in the ownership and operation of industry and agriculture, which generally leads to less inequality in wealth and income than capitalism does.

TABLE 2.9 GOVERNMENT VERSUS PRIVATE OWNERSHIP AND OPERATION

CRITERIA / ALTERNATIVES	C Goal High productivity (C=3 L=1)	L Goal Equity (C=1 L=3)	L Goal Workplace quality (C=1 L=3)	L Goal Environmental protection (C=1 L=3)	L Goal Consumer protection (C=1 L=3)	N Total Neutral weights	L Total Liberal or socialistic weights	C Total Conservative or capitalistic weights
L Alternative Government ownership and operation (socialism)	2	4	2	2	2	24	32*	16
C Alternative Private ownership and operation (capitalism)	4	2	2	2	2	24	28	20*
N Alternative Some government and some private	3	3	2	2	2	18	24	18
S Alternative 100% government ownership and 100% private operation	>3	>3	>3	>3	>3	>30	>39**	>21**

On the goals that relate to the workplace, the environment, and consumers, the socialists traditionally argue that government ownership-operation is more sensitive to those matters because it is less profit oriented. The capitalists traditionally argue that private ownership-operation is more sensitive in competitive marketplaces in order to find quality workers and to increase the quantity of one's consumers. The reality (as contrasted to the theory) is that without alternative incentives or regulations, both government managers and private managers of factories and farms are motivated toward high production at low cost. That kind of motivation leads to cutting back on the expenses of providing workplace quality, environmental protection, and consumer protection. The government factory manager of the Polish steelworks may be just as abusive of labor as the private factory manager of the US Steel Company. Likewise, the government factory managers in the state factories of China may be just as insensitive to consumer safety and durability as their monopolistic counterparts in the American automobile industry.

C. A Super-Optimum Solution

As for how the super-optimum solution operates, it involves government ownership, but all the factories and farms are rented to private entrepreneurs to develop productive and profitable manufacturing and farming. Each lease is renewable every year, or longer if necessary to get productive tenants. A renewal can be refused if the factory or farm is not being productively developed, or if the entrepreneur is not showing adequate sensitivity to workers, the environment, and consumers.

As for some of the advantages of such an SOS system, it is easier to not renew a lease than it is to issue injunctions, fines, jail sentences, or other negative sanctions. It is also much less expensive than subsidies. The money received for rent can be an important source of tax revenue for the government to provide productive subsides elsewhere in the economy. Those subsidies can be especially used for encouraging technological innovation-diffusion, the upgrading of skills, and stimulating competition for market share which can be so much more beneficial to society than either socialistic or capitalistic monopolies. The government can more easily demand sensitivity to workers, the environment, and consumers from its renters of factories and farms than it can from itself. There is a conflict of interest in regulating oneself. Also see Table 2.10 "Simplified Table on Ownership and Operation."

This SOS alternative is mainly available to socialistic countries like Russia, China, Cuba, North Korea, and others since they already own the factories and land. It would not be economically or politically feasible for capitalistic countries to move from the conservative capitalistic alternative to the SOS solution by acquiring ownership through payment or confiscation. This is an example where socialistic countries are in a position to decide between socialism and capitalism by compromising and winding up with the worst of both possible worlds. That means the relative unproductivity of socialism and the relative inequity of capitalism. The socialistic countries are also in a position to decide between the two basic alternatives by winding up with the best of both possible worlds. That means retaining the equities and social sensitivities of government ownership, while having the high productivity that is associated with profit-seeking entrepreneurial capitalism. It would be difficult to find a better example of compromising versus super-optimizing than the current debate over socialism versus capitalism.

Table 2.10 Simplified Table on Ownership and Operation

GOALS / ALTERNATIVES	C High productivity	L Equity
C 1. Government ownership and operation (Socialism)	+	-
L 1. Private ownership and operation (Capitalism)	-	+
N 1. Some government and some private	0	0
SOS OR WIN-WIN 1. 100% government owned and 100% private operation 2. 100% private with government incentives. Both SOSs.	++	++

VI. INFLATION IN RUSSIA

As part of the transition from a communist economy to a free marketplace, a key problem is the inflation which is likely to occur. It occurs for a number of reasons, such as:

1. The lifting of price controls which provide for artificially low prices on essentials like food, shelter, and clothing. The better approach is food stamps, rent supplements, or subsidies rather than price controls.
2. The shortages of goods at least until the private sector can replace the production of the public sector. This may require subsidies to enable would-be entrepreneurs to get started, especially if competition among producers is desired.
3. The tendency on the part of the government to print money in order to meet government payrolls and other expenditures. That tendency is stimulated by the loss of income due to the government turning over income-producing activities to the private sector. In theory, the remedy is to establish new taxes and raise old ones. In practice, one of the prices of democracy is effective public resistance to being taxed. The long-run solution is to increase the gross national product

through well-placed subsidies. Doing so increases the tax base so that relatively low tax rates can bring in more revenue.

A. Alternatives and Goals

Some of these ideas are incorporated into Table 2.11 on "Simplified Table on Inflation and Russia, Starting 1992." The conservative alternative in Russia is to maintain the command economy of price control as much as possible. The liberal position is to establish a free marketplace with a hands-off policy by the government. The compromise position is indexing of wages to cushion the effects of inflation, manipulating interest rates as with the American Federal Reserve system, and decreasing government spending while increasing taxes in accordance with Keynesian theory. Indexing is objected to in Russia on the grounds that it encourages inflation. Raising interest rates does not mean much for reducing inflation in Russia if people are not driving up prices with borrowed money. Reducing government spending and increasing taxes may be even more difficult in Russia than it is in the United States. This is so because of the need for well placed government spending as part of the transition and because the people may be more resistant to being burdened with new taxes than having old taxes raised.

Table 2.11 Simplified Table on Inflation and Russia

GOALS ALTERNATIVES	C Fast stop to inflation	L Fast move to free enterprise
C 1. Command economy (price control)	+	-
L 1. Free marketplace (hands-off)	-	+
N 1. Indexing 2. Interest rates 3. Spending-taxing	0	0
SOS OR WIN-WIN 1. Raise GNP fast by well-placed incentives	++	++

The key conservative goal is to put a fast stop to inflation. The key liberal goal is to facilitate a fast move to free enterprise. On stopping inflation, price controls in a command economy can do that better in the short run than a free marketplace, especially one that has both a shortage of goods and a shortage of competitive producers and sellers. On a fast move to free enterprise, a hands-off policy by the government does that almost by definition, although not necessarily competitive free enterprise. A command economy interferes with free enterprise almost by definition, but that partly depends on what the economy commands.

B. A Three-Part SOS

A super-optimum solution involves raising the GNP fast by well-placed incentives. That means incentives that relate to better marketing, more competition, and more equitable distribution. On the matter of marketing relative to production, the Russian economy is not doing so badly in producing food, housing, clothing, and other essentials, but the products are not getting to the consumers the way they should be. Food is rotting in the fields for lack of adequate storage and transportation facilities. A key reason in the past for spoilage was low controlled prices. Food that is getting out of the fields to the cities may then rot in warehouses for lack of a well organized retailing system. Communist Russia drove out a high percentage of its retail businessmen in the early years and drove out their sons and daughters in more recent years. Communist Russia as of 1917 was comparable to medieval Spain in 1492 in driving out the Arab. Jewish, and other merchants. Both places went downhill thereafter. Russia, however, is in a position through well-placed subsidies (including training subsidies) to stimulate a new entrepreneurial class.

On the matter of more competition, it was an enriching experience to hear one of the leaders of the Communist Party of the Soviet Union speak at a conference at the Russian Academy of Sciences on the need for a competitive free market. His position was that the Communist Party had no objection as of 1990 to private ownership and operation of the means of production and distribution. They did, however, object to putting those facilities into the hands of national, regional, and local monopolists. In that sense, the Communist Party was preaching a doctrine of competitive capitalism more akin to Adam Smith than either Marxist-Leninists or American conservatives. Both Marx and Lenin objected to monopolies, but thought that government ownership would show sensitivity to workers and consumers that private monopolies do not. That was a bit naive in view of the abuse of workers by such government-owned entities as the Polish steel mills, or the abuse of consumers by such government-owned entities as public power companies. Likewise, American conservatives tend to be quite supportive of monopolistic power companies, as opposed to the competitive system of the New Deal whereby the Tennessee Valley Authority and other publicly owned power companies would serve as competitive yardsticks.

It is one thing to say that competition is desirable. It is another thing to bring it about. It does not occur through natural forces or invisible hands, as indicated by the increasing monopolization of the American economy through business mergers. It also does not occur through anti-trust penalties since both conservative and liberal governments are reluctant to break up what they consider to be efficient big businesses using economies of scale. The Japanese Ministry of International Trade and Industry may have an ideal modern approach of combining privatization with competition. The MITI gives subsidies to Japanese firms in such industries as automobiles, electronics, and computers. It does so in such a way as to guarantee multiple Japanese firms in all those industries, rather than a single monopolistic giant or two or three oligopolistic giants. Well-placed subsidies in Russia could deliberately encourage the development of competing firms. Such competition results in lower prices, better quality goods, and better workplaces to attract workers.

The third area for well-placed subsidies is to guarantee more equitable distribution. Private enterprise is not likely to want to provide unprofitable mail service to isolated rural families. The publicly owned post office is willing to do so. A private enterprise, though, would also be willing to do so with a well-placed equity subsidy assuming society feels that there should be rural mail service. That is more efficient than forcing the price of postage below a profitable level across the country causing private mail delivery and other enterprises to want to sell out to the government. It makes more sense in terms of prices that operate within the laws of supply and demand to let the price of food and housing rise or fall in accordance with those forces. Food stamps and rent vouchers can be provided to those who otherwise would not eat or go homeless.

C. Tabular or Spreadsheet Analysis

Thus with a system of well-placed incentives to improve marketing, competition, and equitable distribution, the Russian economy could reduce inflation, especially inflation that is due to shortages of goods and monopolistic pricing. The effect may not be as great in the short run as price control, but it avoids black markets and is better in the long run. Likewise, such a system of incentives can move the economy fast toward free enterprise, especially competitive free enterprise that the public will accept and even welcome. The effect on free enterprise may not be as great in the short run as a total hands-off policy, but the incentives system avoids the unfree system in the long run of monopolistic control with inflated prices. See Table 2-12 "Inflation and Russia, Starting 1992."

Tables 2.11 and 2.12 both illustrate how the super-optimum alternative can be a loser on every goal and still be an overall winner. Being that kind of a loser means not coming out in first place on any of the goals, but generally running contrary to the tradeoff idea that if an alternative does well on some goals, then it must do not so well on other goals. All we need are alternatives that are generally on the positive side on a 1-5 scale, which means doing better than a 3. Such an alternative is then likely to score higher on the liberal totals than the liberal alternative, which does poorly on the conservative goals. The SOS alternative is also likely to score higher on the conservative totals than the conservative alternative, which does poorly on the liberal goals.

TABLE 2.12 INFLATION AND RUSSIA, STARTING 1992

CRITERIA \ ALTERNATIVES	C GOAL Fast Stop to Inflation C=3 N=2 L=1	·L· GOAL Fast Move to Free Enterprise C=1 N=2 L=3	N TOTAL (Neutral Weights)	L TOTAL (Liberal Weights)	C TOTAL (Conservative Weights)
C ALTERNATIVE Command Economy (Price Control)	4	2	12	10	14*
L ALTERNATIVE Free Marketplace (Hands-Off)	2	4	12	14*	10
N ALTERNATIVE Indexing, Interest Rates, Spending-Taxing	3	3	12	12	12
S ALTERNATIVE Raise GNP Fast by Well-Placed Incentives	≥ 3.5	≥ 3.5	≥ 12	$\geq 14**$	$\geq 14**$

Note:

The SOS incentives are designed to stimulate:

(1) Better marketing

(2) More competition

(3) More equitable distribution through vouchers for food, clothes, and housing.

D. Some Conclusions

Overall conclusions can be derived from this analysis in terms of the substance of what is involved in the transition from socialism to capitalism in Russia and Eastern Europe.

1. Avoid Extreme Capitalism

Do not go to the opposite extreme of adopting a form of capitalism that capitalistic United States would consider to be too far in a right-wing conservative direction. The American federal government owns lots of land, especially in the western United States. It would be virtually unthinkable in American politics for the federal government to give the land away to private business, or even to sell a place like Yosemite National Park for private commercial development. It is not unthinkable, though, for the federal government to lease federal land for grazing, farming, or other development. It is likewise not unthinkable to award franchises to private entrepreneurs to sell products in Yosemite National Park.

The American federal government even (and maybe especially) during the conservative Reagan administration did not have a hands-off policy regarding the American economy. Reagan sought to make use of well-placed subsidies in the form of enterprise zones to attract business firms to the inner cities, and housing vouchers as a way of providing equity in the housing market.

2. Avoid the Middle Way and the Mixed-Up Economy

Do not go to the so-called middle way that is associated with places like Sweden or the mixed economies of Western Europe. It may provide the worst of both possible worlds, rather than the best. This shows up in government versus private ownership and operation. The middle way of the mixed economy provides lots of production and distribution exclusively by the private sector and other production and distribution exclusively by the public sector. Each sector may operate monopolistically with insensitivity to workers, consumers, and the environment. This is contrasted with the super-optimum system of having title to the property in the government with a renewable lease for private development, subject to non-renewal for violating the rights of workers, consumers, or the environment.

This also shows up in the command economy versus the laissez-faire marketplace. The mixed economy involves some products that are subject to price control like rents in New York City, or the price of food in Africa. The prices of other products are allowed to rise and fall in accordance with the market. The controlled prices result in shortages. The market prices result in exploitation. Both undesirable occurrences can be avoided by (1) letting all prices rise and fall in accordance with the market, and (2) having well-placed subsidies to provide for (a) a more efficient market and marketing, (b) plus competition, and (c) plus equity for those who cannot meet the market prices.

VII. FOREIGN OWNERSHIP OF STOCK IN POLAND

Should Poland when it goes to selling stock in corporations allow foreigners to freely buy stock, or have some limits on how much stock can be owned by foreigners? That was a good tradeoff problem. See Table 2.13 "Polish Corporate Stock." The conservative position was not to sell any stock to foreigners. It was conservative in the sense of preserving the communist system, not conservative in the sense of pro-capitalist. The fear was that Poland would be exploited by Americans. But yet it was privatization in the sense that the people would own, stock and not have state-owned factories. The liberal position was let anybody buy the stock who has the money to pay for it, even though it would mean that Americans might have controlling interests in Polish corporations. The neutral position would be to let foreigners buy the stock up to 49% so that Poland could benefit from their dollars but not lose control. Actually they would lose control possibly selling 20% if the 20% sticks together and the other 80% does not show much interest in voting their stock rights. The basic goals are to get money, i.e., to get capital for development, to democratize the decision-making, or to avoid foreign exploitation.

Table 2.13. Polish Corporate Stock

GOALS ⟍ ALTERNATIVES	C Avoid foreign exploitation	L Get capital for development
C 1. Retain stock in Poland	+	-
L 1. Let all buy	-	+
N 1. Up to 49%	0	0
SOS OR WIN-WIN 1. Poland retains little 2. Leases to corporate entrepreneurs	++	++

Retaining the stock only in Poland is not so good for getting capital, although good for avoiding foreign exploitation. The democratic decision-making is a goal that is not maybe so relevant to the issue of foreigners versus domestic people buying stock. It is more relevant to the issue that had already been decided, namely that the companies would be owned by individuals as stockholders rather than as state-owned enterprises. If democratic decision-making means control by the Polish people, then that is the same thing as avoiding foreign exploitation. If democratic decision-making means being controlled by people regardless if they are Polish or otherwise, then it does not make any difference. Especially since the Americans who are likely to invest in Poland are probably going to be disproportionately Polish Americans. Actually, the foreign exploitation as of 1992 versus about 1986 when this came up might now mean a fear of Japan taking over. They have more money to invest in E. Europe if they want to do so than the United States might have. Or a worse fear, namely that Germany is going to take over, which is a much more emotional subject than Japan or the United States.

The super-optimum solution might be the arrangement whereby the government retains title and turns over the development of the steel mill or whatever it is to private enterprise, which then sells stock to whoever wants to buy its stock. In other words, the steel mills at Gdansk get turned over to the Mitsubishi Company, or U. S. Steel, or Germany Steel, to run efficiently. This probably would not mean U.S. Steel. All of those are corporations that sell stock. In turning the franchise to run the steel mill or the lease over to Mitsubishi, it could be provided for in the lease that Mitsubishi must give a discount to Polish buyers in buying stock in Mitsubishi, that they get 10% or 20% off whatever the selling price is. Most of Mitsubishi's stock is not sold by the Mitsubishi Company, it is sold in a stock market by previous owners who are selling to new owners. Mitsubishi has no control over what they sell for. Mitsubishi does every once in a while sell a new issue of stock that no one has previously owned. The lease can specify that there must be a new issue of stock to cover the capital for the Polish steel mills and on that new issue of stock there should be a 20% discount to Polish citizens to encourage more domestic ownership. That may not be sufficient, partly because any non-Polish citizens who want to own some of the stock can arrange for Polish citizens to be front men for them in order to benefit from the discount. The answer is let Mitsubishi sell the stock to anybody at the market price reflecting supply and demand. Poland will retain control to prevent foreign exploitation not by having a bunch of Polish stockholders who are front men or who are truly Polish citizens but do not care about going to corporation meetings, they just want dividends, or worse just want to resell the stock at a profit. Instead, the Polish government has the realistic authority to not renew the lease if Mitsubishi is doing exploitative things like providing unsafe workplaces, polluting the environment, or being a bad corporate citizen in some other way like cheating on taxes. That is the best control, not control through stockholders.

That would be a SOS with regard to having a positive effect on getting capital is provided for development. Also, more democratic decision-making than any kind of stockholder arrangement since it establishes political control rather than stockholder control. It is political control in that it is a responsibility of the government of Poland to prevent violation of Polish laws, not a responsibility of the stockholders who might even welcome violation of the Polish laws if they can make more profit on resale or dividends. If the government is not exercising its power to not renew leases, then that could be used in a democratic system by the opposition party to get votes to throw out the prevailing government. It is much easier in the United States to throw out the president every four years than it is to throw out the head of GM who can do no right and still be retained and given raises.

If President Bush or Clinton operated like the presidents of General Motors do, he might risk impeachment, not just non-reelection. There is far more accountability of government people in a democracy than there is of corporate people in a democracy. Political democracy has very little spillover to corporate government. They operate just as authoritarian under a dictatorship as they do under a democracy. They are living in a different world on a different track. The title and leasing approach democratizes corporate management in providing for a more meaningful ultimate political decision-making. One could say that Congress could always pass a law changing the way in which General Motors operates with regard to some things, such as pass a law that totally wipes out all tariffs and quotas on imported automobiles. That still would not necessarily bring about any change in the operations of GM, just more complaining about cheating. International cheating seems to be the new bogey man for a certain segment of the right wing. They cannot scream communist conspiracy. They cannot accuse Japan of being uncapitalistic, undemocratic, or inefficient. On the third goal, it is definitely more effective than the conservative or liberal alternatives on avoiding exploitation. It may not raise as much capital as letting anybody buy. But it is an overall SOS in that it does better on the set of three goals than the conservative alternative does on the conservative totals or the liberal alternative does on the liberal totals.

VIII. REFERENCES FOR FURTHER RELEVANT READING

On policy problems in post-1945 China, see William Jones (ed.), *Basic Principles of Civil Law in China* (Armonk, N.Y.: M. E. Sharpe, 1989); Harry Harding, *China's Second Revolution: Reform After Mao* (Washington, D.C.: Brookings Institution, 1987); John Burns and Stanley Rosen (eds.), *Policy Conflicts in Post-Mao China* (Armonk, N.Y.: M.E. Sharpe, 1986); and John Major and Anthony Kane (eds.), *China Briefing* (Boulder, Colo.: Westview Press, 1987).

On increasing productivity in the public and private sectors, see Marc Holzer and S. Nagel (eds.), *Productivity and Public Policy* (Sage, 1984); Rita Mae Kelly (ed.), *Promoting Productivity in the Public Sector: Problems, Strategies, and Prospects* (St. Martin's, 1988); Marc Holzer and Arie Halachmi, *Public Sector Productivity: A Resource Guide* (Garland, 1988); Michael LeBoeuf, *The Productivity Challenge: How to Make it Work for America and You* (McGraw Hill. 1982); and Ryuzo Sato and Gilbert Suzawa, *Research and Productivity: Endogenous Technical Change* (Auburn House, 1983).

For books specifically on inflation reduction without increasing unemployment especially in the context of Eastern Europe, see Paul Peretz, *The Political Economy of Inflation in the United States* (University of Chicago Press, 1983); Kreisky Commission on Employment Issues in Europe, *A Programme for Full Employment in the 1990s* (Pergamon Press, 1989); and Laszlo Cwaba (ed.), *Systemic Change and Stabilization in Eastern Europe* (Dartmouth. 1991).

Chapter 3

TECHNOLOGY POLICY CONTROVERSIES

I. TRANSPORTATION POLICY: BICYCLES VERSUS CARS IN BEIJING

The most exciting presentations in China were those that involved systematic policy analysis, decision-aiding software, multi-criteria decision-making, and super-optimum solutions. One example was the problem of how to deal with the substantial and increasing quantity of night-time accidents involving cars crashing into bicycles in Beijing and other Chinese cities. There are over seven million bicycles in Beijing, which is more bicycles in Beijing than there are people in any American city except Los Angeles and New York.

The material which follows briefly describes how one might systematically analyze the basic alternatives available for dealing with the problem, the goals or criteria for choosing among the alternatives, and relations between alternatives and goals in order to choose or explain the best alternative, combination, allocation, or predictive decision-rule.

The material which follows includes both a verbal analysis and a computer output. The computer output involves a matrix or table of columns and rows in which the goals are on the columns, the alternatives are on the rows, the relations between goals and alternatives are in the cells, the overall score for each alternative is at the far right, and the system provides for doing an analysis whereby one can determine what it would take to bring a second-place alternative or other-place alternative up to first place. See Table 3.1 "The Problem of Collisions between Bicycles and Cars."

TABLE 3.1 THE PROBLEM OF COLLISIONS BETWEEN BICYCLES AND CARS

CRITERIA / ALTERNATIVES	L Goal +Safety	C Goal ·Cost	L Goal Equity	N Goal Political Feasibil.	N Goal Admin. Feasibil.	N Total Neutral weights	L Total Liberal weights	C Total Conserv. weights
L Alternative Reflectors	4	3				14	15	13
L Alternative Lights	5	1				12	16*	8
C Alternative Do Nothing	2	4				12	10	14*
C Alternative No Night Bikes	5.1	1		1	1	12.2	16.3	8.1
L Alternative Free Reflectors	4.1	2.5	4			21.2	25.8*	15.6
C Alternative Buy Reflectors	3.9	3.5	2			18.8	21.2	16.4*
L Alternative Require Manufacturer	4.3	3.7				16	16.6*	15.4*
C Alternative Subsidize Manufacturer	4.5	2.3				13.6	15.8	11.4
S Alternative SOS	5.1	4.5	5			19.2	19.8**	18.6**

NOTES:

1. C = conservative; L = liberal; N = neutral; and S = super-optimum solution.
    *Conservative or liberal winner without the SOS.
    **Conservative or liberal winner considering the SOS.

2. The benefits of increasing safety include reducing injuries, reducing traffic disruption, and reducing ambulance costs. The components of the cost variable include equipment costs and enforcement costs, and interference costs. Scores are not shown on those goals because they are subgoals of the main goals of safety and cost, although scores could be shown if one wants further details.

3. Scores on the equity goal are only shown and added for comparing free reflectors with buying reflectors since that is where the equity goal is mainly involved. Likewise, scores on the feasibility goals are only shown for prohibiting bicycles at night since that alternative is not politically or administratively feasible.

A. The Inputs

1. The Alternatives

1. Having reflectors on bicycles in order to decrease the increase in the number of nighttime accidents between cars and bicycles.
2. Having battery-operated lights on bicycles. The word "having" for alternatives 1 and 2 means requiring by law.
3. This is the alternative of doing nothing, just leaving things the way they are.
4. This involves prohibiting bicycles at night.
5. This involves giving away the reflectors free at government expense instead of having people buy the reflectors.
6. This involves having people buy the reflectors. Thus, alternatives 5 and 6 are subdivisions of alternative 1 which just talks about requiring reflectors but doesn't clarify who is going to pay for them.
7. This is requiring manufacturers and sellers of bicycles to put reflectors on them before they sell them.
8. This involves subsidizing manufacturers to get them to put reflectors on bicycles.
9. Requiring manufacturers in the future to use reflective paint on bicycles so that the bicycles can be seen better at night by cars than either reflectors or lights provide. Using a reflective paint costs no more than using regular paint. There is no extra cost involved but a lot of extra benefits.

2. The Criteria

1. Reduce the number of accidents, especially where there are fatalities or personal injuries or even just property damage.
2. Keep the cost down to the taxpayer and to society.
3. The third especially important criterion is equity, meaning avoid solutions that unduly burden the poor. Stated more positively, seek solutions that do not discriminate against any major groups of people in terms of who benefits and who pays the costs. Criteria 3, 4, 5 all relate to benefits that came from reducing bicycle-car injuries. Number 3 has to do with the cost to the injured person and to the economy as a result of that person's productivity being lost.
4. That is the cost with regard to the disruption of traffic that could cause tie-ups where everybody is late for wherever they are going.
5. That is the cost to the government to send out an ambulance or a police car to take a police report. Items 3, 4, and 5 are benefit items in the sense that if injuries are reduced then the benefits of no lost productivity or lost medical costs are saved and no lost disruption of traffic or lost governmental involvement.
6. These are 3 subdivisions of the cost that are expressed in number 2 above. One cost has to do with the cost of equipment such as what it would cost people to buy reflectors versus lights with batteries.
7. This is the cost of enforcement since some solutions require more police enforcement than others.

8. This is the cost of interference with the economy and productivity as a result of such solutions as prohibiting bicycles at night.
9. Equity as mentioned above.
10. This is political feasibility since different proposals have different degrees of likelihood of being adopted and some have no likelihood at all.
11. This is administrative feasibility since some proposals like prohibiting bicycles at night may be almost administratively impossible even if the proposal is adopted.

3. The Data Matrix

Looking at the greater detail from the data matrix, first going down the injuries column from the highest to the lowest.

1. Reflective paint does best.
2. Then comes battery-operated light.
3. Then comes subsidized reflectors put on by the manufacturer.
4. Then requiring manufacturers and sellers to put on reflectors.
5. Then comes free reflectors for existing bicycles.
6. Then comes requiring people to buy reflectors.
7. A distant last is keeping things as they are.
8. Since there are 9 altogether, 2 must have been left out. One is reflectors in general that does worse on reducing injuries than lights but is less expensive than lights.
9. Also left out was prohibiting bicycles at night, which would be near the top with regard to reducing injuries if it could be adopted and enforced. See Table 3.1 for the data matrix that relates the nine alternatives to the three main goals.

B. The Outputs

The overall winner is to give free reflectors for existing bicycles but require manufacturers and seller to put reflectors on future bicycles at their own expense without a subsidy.

That is the combination solution before considering the SOS which outscores every alternative on every criterion, at least for long-run adoption, namely the reflective point. It is a long-run solution but there would be a lot of existing bicycles that would need to be taken care of in the meantime. Therefore, the best solution would be free reflectors for existing bicycles and requiring reflective paint for all future bicycles rather than requiring reflectors for future bicycles which are more expensive and less effective.

The Beijing bicycle problem thus illustrates such broader aspects of public policy evaluation as (1) the role of effectiveness, efficiency, and equity as goals, (2) the importance of considering political and administrative feasibility, (3) the use of 1-5 scales for expressing relations between alternatives and goals, (4) the need for dealing with multiple measurement on multiple goals, (5) the usefulness of threshold analysis in dealing with both multi-dimensionally and missing information, (6) using subsidies to increase compliance with law, (7) the nature of a dominating SOS solution which does better than the other alternatives on all the goals, (8) working with groups of criteria, (9) working with groups of alternatives, and (10) the importance of working with realistic problems.

II. Trying to Commute to and from Manila

The Manila commuting problem is a good example of how people in developed countries may have false stereotypes of policy problems in developing countries being simpler and less urbanized than policy problems in more developed countries. There may be no country in the world that has a worse commuter problem than the Philippines. Commuting is relatively simple in New York, London, Paris, Berlin, Moscow, Tokyo, and elsewhere.

It is more complicated in the Philippines because:

1. The Philippines has only one really big metropolitan city to which people are flocking, whereas countries like the United States have many such cities like New York, Chicago, Los Angeles, etc.
2. Metropolitan Manila may be bigger in population and area than most other big cities where there is a lot of complaining about the difficulty of commuting. Metropolitan Manila consists of about five adjacent cities, including Quezon City which is a big city in itself.
3. Greatly complicating the commuting problem in Manila is that it is on an island or a peninsula in which the Pacific Ocean is just waiting to flood any attempt to build a subway system. Further complicating matters is the lack of money for an expanded elevated or surface train system.
4. It has been proposed that there should be more vehicles that carry multiple people to and from work to ease the commuting problem. Washington, D.C., for example, makes a big thing of providing special lanes for cars and buses that have multiple passengers, especially as part of a pooling arrangement. The Manila area probably has more small buses per capita than any city in the world. They have developed a mass transit system based on the extended jeep carrying a dozen or more passengers crowded closely together.
5. Having more jeepneys, small buses, and big buses would just further clog the highways and streets into and out of Manila. They would thus worsen the problem and make commuting even more time-consuming.
6. Having more bicycles will not handle the Manila commuter problem the way it helps in Beijing. Poor people and middle-class people have too far to travel to do it on bicycle, and they can also ride the jeepney buses for only one peso which is about 1/20 of an American dollar. It thus is not cost-effective to buy and ride a bicycle to work. The more influential car drivers would also not tolerate giving up an auto land on each side of the streets to be used by bicycles.

7. This commuting phenomenon is not peculiar to the Philippines as a developing country. Many developing countries have a capital city or central city to which rural people are flocking looking for jobs. The people build whatever shanties they can. The city becomes highly over-crowded, not just relative to the jobs available, but in an absolute sense given the limited space and the limited technological capabilities of moving people around in that limited space.

A. Alternatives

Table 3.2 shows the Manila commuter problem in the context of a decision analysis table or a super-optimizing framework. The conservative alternative (as is often the case) is to leave things as they are, or leave it up to the marketplace to change things. Some conservatives like to talk about people buying cities the way they buy products. In that sense, people supposedly vote with their feet by going to Manila. The invisible hand of Adam Smith may eventually cause them to change their votes and go back to the countryside. That runs contrary to the invisible hand of somebody else who said something about once you have tasted the big city it is hard to go back to the farm, especially if the landless peasants have no farm to go back to. Maybe in the extremely long run, things get so bad in overcrowded cities that medieval diseases return to periodically decimate the population. That fortunately or unfortunately is not so likely given modern public health care.

TABLE 3.2 MANILA COMMUTER PROBLEM

CRITERIA / ALTERNATIVES	L Goal -Time commuting	C Goal -Taxes	N Total Neutral weights	L Total Liberal weights	C Total Conservative weights
C Alternative Leave as it is	1	4	10	7	13*
L Alternative Mass Transit	4	2	12	14*	10
N Alternative Hodgepodge: more jeepneys and buses	2	2.5	9	8.5	9.5
S Alternative Suburbs, regional cities, overseas, and other employment centers	4.5	4.5	18	18**	18**

The liberal solution tends to be spending big money, but often with no strings attached and with an unduly narrow focus on the immediate problem, rather than the bigger picture. Liberals also tend to project their middle-class New York or Chicago values on poor people, rural people, and people in developing countries. In this context, it means proposing a New York or Chicago subway or elevated line or Washington, D.C. car pooling. Those alternatives were mentioned above as not so applicable to Manila and maybe not so applicable to most developing countries for lack of capital. The available capital could probably be better spent in upgrading human skills and machinery for producing goods. It should also be noted that at least some developing countries may be in a good position to act fast in time to prevent a good deal of urban congestion, rather than try to cure it or commute it afterward.

The neutral alternative as in many situations tends to involve splitting the difference between conservative expenditures or recommendations and those of the liberals. If the conservatives say spend nothing on mass transit (since it will overburden the taxpayer and may encourage people to move to Manila), and if the liberals say spend many millions, then the neutral compromisers try to find a figure in between. Doing so may result in half of a train system and may be an example of where half a loaf is worse than none. A half-way system could be expensive without adequate incremental benefits. Neutrals also tend to emphasize trying a lot of things simultaneously. In this context, that would mean a little more jeepneys, small buses, big buses, bicycles, and subsidized taxis. The result would probably be more congestion and more commuting-time wasted, as mentioned above. Building wider highways for the additional vehicles is also not likely to help. Many of the commuting roads in Manila are already much wider than Chicago's Outer Drive. The ultimate would be to clear out all the buildings, and have nothing but commuting roads.

B. Goals

As for goals, a key goal is to reduce the tremendous amount of time wasted getting to and from work. Only the richest of Filipinos can afford to live near the central city, or the poorest who set up illegal shanties in whatever alley might be available. The people who live in those shanties frequently do not have jobs to commute to, and neither do the people who live in the rich villas. The working people tend to live substantial distances away, and they may spend approximately two exhausting hours getting into central Manila and then getting out. Those hours are literally exhausting because the exhaust fumes are unbelievable due to the stop-and go operation of many diesel-fueled vehicles and propane buses. Many of the drivers and street vendors wear handkerchiefs over their faces.

Delays are also caused by numerous trucks going to and from factories that are in the central city, along with office buildings. Delay is also caused by many beggars and street vendors who interfere with traffic at intersections. A further factor is having large military barracks in the central city that could be used for residential housing. Camp Aguinaldo, which is one of the leading army camps in the Philippines, is in downtown

Manila. Americans reading about soldiers from Camp Aguinaldo invading the Makati business district think they may have come as paratroopers. The soldiers simply walked down the block into the high-rise buildings. The hot climate further adds to the problem by making the commuting less bearable and causing a lot of over-heated cars that stall and block traffic.

The second key goal is to keep the tax burden down. On the matter of tax burden, though, one has to distinguish between the short run burden and the long-run burden. The long-run (if it is not too far away) is more important since it lasts longer. In this context, it may be necessary to spend a lot of money to do something about the problem in order to save a lot of time-cost later. More important, by enabling people in the Manila area to be more productive and healthy, the gross national product may benefit substantially, thereby increasing the tax base. If that happens then the percentage tax rate can be subsequently lowered and still bring in more money for other projects.

Saving commuting time for workers tends to be a relatively liberal goal, and saving tax money for taxpayers tends to be a relatively conservative goal. As with other SOS analyses, however, both liberals and conservatives endorse time-saving and tax-saving. It is just a matter of the relative emphasis of liberals compared to conservatives.

C. Scoring and Totals

In scoring the alternatives, leaving things as they are is terrible for saving commuting time, but it does have a positive relation with short-run tax saving. Spending a lot of money on a train system that would run through developed areas of Manila or on a median strip of widened highways could save commuting time, but it does have a negative relation with short-run tax saving. The neutral compromise is not much help on saving time, although it is not as bad as doing nothing. Likewise it does have a short-run incremental tax burden, although not as bad as liberal mass-transit expenditures.

Looking at the totals, the conservative alternative comes in first using the conservative weights, with the liberal alternative in third place. Likewise the liberal alternative comes in first using the liberal weights, with the conservative alternative in third place. The neutral alternative is everybody's second. It is possibly even the second or third choice of the neutrals since the hodgepodge-neutral alternative does poorly on both goals, although it is not the worst on both goals. In arriving at a super-optimum solution, the important thing is finding an alternative that exceeds both the liberal and conservative initial best expectations, not necessarily the neutrals.

D. The Super-Optimum Solution

The super-optimum solution in this context has at least three parts. The first is to build up employment opportunities in the suburbs or outlying portions of Manila. The commuting is highly unbalanced. It is nearly all inward in the morning starting about 5:00 in the morning, and it is nearly all outward in the evening starting at about 3:00. This is unlike American cities where there is an increasing growth in the suburbs as places for employment opportunities, not just bedrooms. Farmland northwest of Chicago in places like Schaumberg Township now have skyscraper office buildings and low-pollution factories.

As a concrete example, it is amazing that the University of the Philippines which is located in Quezon City outside of Manila does not have a high-tech area around it. That would take advantage of the fact that the University is the leading university in the Philippines and possibly the leading university in Southeast Asia. Most American universities that have engineering schools attract high-tech employment in their areas. The Philippine government could provide subsidies to create a high-tech employment area around the university. This would make a dent in the commuting problem, and set a useful precedent for other subsidized suburban employment. Also important is that it would help subsidize technological innovation and diffusion. Doing so could have broader useful effects on the Philippine economy than just the Manila commuter problem.

The second part of a possible super-optimum solution is subsidizing the development of regional cities throughout the Philippines. Certain cities in the southern provinces of Mindanao and the middle provinces between Manila and Mindanao could be made more attractive to rural people from those provinces as places to migrate to, rather than go to Manila. They could even be made attractive enough possibly to get some people to move from Manila back to those regional cities in their home provinces. This is a kind of subsidization that has been done in the Soviet Union to encourage people to move west. It was also done by the United States to encourage people to move west, although more a matter of providing people with land for farming in the west, rather than urban employment opportunities. The Rural Rehabilitation Administration during the 1930's, however, did provide low interest loans to enable rural people from Oklahoma, Arkansas, and elsewhere in the southwest to go to Los Angeles and establish gas stations and other small businesses or become automobile mechanics, rather than go to Chicago, Detroit, Cleveland, and New York, as was the case with poor southern blacks and whites.

The third part of the solution might be for the Philippine government to work more actively with a number of other governments that have labor shortages who could hire some of the excess labor in the Manila area and other parts of the Philippines. This may be true of Hong Kong, Singapore, Taiwan, Malaysia, Korea, and even Japan. It might be worthwhile for the Philippine government to do more to upgrade labor skills to make that kind of guest-worker program more attractive. Those guest workers also send back lots of money to help the Philippine economy, which may be even more important than relieving the Manila commuter problem. The Philippine government has developed labor-exporting relations with Arab countries on the Persian Gulf. The Philippines Airlines may stop at more Persian Gulf cities as a result than almost any other non-Arab airline. This is another illustration of the need for elevating some of the policy problems of individual countries to a more international or global level.

With that kind of three-part super-optimum solution, commuting time could be substantially reduced, more so than doing nothing, having a mildly effective train system, or a hodgepodge of miscellaneous vehicles rivaling the evacuation of Dunkirk every morning and evening in Manila. Likewise, that kind of super-optimum solution could not only save taxes in the long run by increasing the GNP and the tax base, but it could also help resolve lots of other policy problems besides the Manila commuter problem. An increased GNP through suburban employment, regional cities, and overseas employment can do wonders with regard to reducing the problems of crime, poverty, discrimination, and lack of money for education, health care, housing, and other public policy expenditures. The SOS does show up in Table 3.2 as being a substantial winner on the liberal, conservative, and neutral totals. That includes winning over the previous liberal and conservative alternatives or expectations even with liberal and conservative weights. Also see Table 3.3 "Simplified Table on the Commuter Problem."

Table 3.3 Simplified Table On Commuter Problem

GOALS ALTERNATIVES	C Decrease taxes	L Decrease time commuting
C As is	+	-
L Mass transit	-	+
N Hodge podge with more jeepneys and buses	0	0
SOS OR WIN-WIN Suburbs, regional cities, overseas, and other employment centers	++	++

III. SUPER-OPTIMIZING ANALYSIS AND INDIA INDUSTRIAL POLICY

Super-optimizing refers to a new and useful form of public policy evaluation. It seeks to find solutions to policy problems whereby conservatives, liberals, and other major viewpoints can all come out ahead of their best initial expectations simultaneously. The problem of industrial policy can serve as an illustration, including the more specific problem of hand-crafted work versus assembly lines in India.

A. Background and Trends

India's textile policy and the informal sectors is almost an emotional topic in India because it goes to a key part of Gandhiism. He is often pictured making things at a handloom in the informal sector in order to put down the idea of people working in textile factories like the ones that exist in North Carolina. There are statistics with regard to how well the handlooms are completing with the India mills.

If one compares 1912 with 1939, the Indian mills went from about a million yards to 4 million yards. The handlooms went from a million yards to a million and a half. However, if one looks at the more recent figures, something changed. As of 1989, the mills are producing less than they were in 1939. They have dropped from 3.6 to 2.6 and the informal sector has shot up from 1.5 to 10.7. Yet the data shows in 1980 there were 452 power looms and only 15 in 1942, and 944 in 1989. If they have so many more power looms, why are the power looms not producing more cloth?

The conclusion is partly that Gandhiism is working psychologically. There has been a phenomenal expansion of informal handloom output partly for ideological reasons. Probably no other developing nation has that kind of development. It does show that people can get satisfaction out of things that may not be so productive but are probably more fun to do. Working on a textile mill assembly line in North Carolina is pictured in the Norma Rae movie as being very depressing, as contrasted to being one's own boss with the family loom.

This could be generalized a bit. There is no question that highly mechanized collective farms in Russia are not as productive as a bunch of farmers working their own plots as their own boss on into the night. Certain occupations or industries in certain cultures may be more productive by trying to take into consideration individual psychology more instead of treating people like machines.

If the mills were capable of running solely by themselves, like Japanese mills where there is no dehumanizing because there are not many humans around, then one gets a kind of super-optimum solution of high productivity and no dehumanizing. The North Carolina mills which are like the India mills may give the worst of both possible worlds. They may be an example of a super malimum where productivity is down for lack of incentive, and dehumanizing is up due to regimentation. The India handloom is very humanizing, but is not as productive as the Japanese automated factory.

This is relevant to the section of Africa business development. At the 1991 Seychelles conference, that was one of the best debated subjects. Some people lauded the informal sector. Others said that it was only justifiable as a means toward more efficient factories and should not be considered as an end in itself but just a steppingstone.

There has been a big increase in the total productivity of household looms in India versus factory looms. At first, that seems rather strange. The explanation is that the household looms are not handlooms. They are machines, like sewing machines. They run on electricity. They constitute a compromise between home handicrafts and factory machines. These are home machines. They may seem like an ideal compromise. They may, however, sacrifice some potential productivity that could come from more factory automation. They may also sacrifice some equity and quality workplace that could come from home handicrafts, or more likely from a highly automated assembly plant.

B. Alternatives, Goals, and Relations

Table 3.4 "Handwork versus Assembly Lines in India Clothmaking" is a super-optimizing or SOS table. SOS stands for super-optimum solutions. The table shows goals to be achieved on the columns, alternatives available for achieving them on the rows, and indicators of relations between goals and alternatives in the cells. It also shows neutral, liberal, and conservative totals in the columns at the right. Those totals reflect neutral, liberal, and conservative weights for the goals. This is a simplified SOS table. It only involves two goals and four alternatives. Other SOS tables may involve more goals and more alternatives.

TABLE 3.4 HANDWORK VERSUS ASSEMBLY LINE IN INDIA CLOTHMAKING

CRITERIA ALTERNATIVES	C Goal Productivity C=3 N=2 L=1	L Goal Quality Workplace L=3 N=2 C=1	N Total (Neutral Weights)	L Total (Liberal Weights)	C Total (Conservative Weights)
C Alternative Hand-Crafted Work	2	4	12	10	14*
L Alternative Assembly Line Work	4	2	12	14*	10
N Alternative Cottage Industry with Small Machines	3	3	12	12	12
S Alternative Highly Automated Assembly Plant	>3.5 ~5	>3.5 ~5	>12	>14**	>14**

This India problem lends itself well to a simplified SOS. The conservative alternative is handcrafted work by artisans, or just handcrafted work. The liberal approach is a kind of Eli Whitney-Henry Ford assembly line that at one time was considered such a technological advance, which it was. The compromise is the current India situation which involves cottage industry using small machines.

We should say home industry rather than cottage industry, although both sound like they could refer to sweatshops. That is one of the drawbacks to this kind of compromise. It easily leads to people working at home, but they are not their own bosses. They may be more wage slaves than if they worked in a factory. They do piecework, and someone shows up every day or so to pick up what they have done. They get paid a pittance and work all the time. Just because they are at home does not mean that they have much quality of life or control over their hours. The problem is not solved by trying to find a new word for cottage industry or home industry. Whatever it is, it could become a sweatshop. The India data does not say anything about the quality of life of these people working at home. It just says they are producing a lot of cloth. Which may have also been true of the sweatshops in the New York garment industry in the early 1900's.

The conservative goal is productivity. Turn out a lot of cloth at a relatively low price. The liberal goal is a quality workplace in terms of (1) safety, (2) psychologically pleasant, (3) not polluted, and (4) with work that is not drudgery.

The handcrafted work involves a quality workplace. It is pretty hard to do much polluting when one works with needle and thread. It is also pretty hard to get an arm chopped off by a power tool when one works with needle and thread. On the productivity side though, needle and thread is not so productive.

Assembly line work one would expect would be more productive than cottage industry with small machines. However, if there are a lot of homes with a lot of small machines, they will out produce a small quantity of assembly lines. Even though one assembly line produces a lot more than one home. It depends on how we define productivity. If it is defined in terms of effectiveness or total output, then the India data shows the home industry is doing better. If productivity means output divided by some kind of input of money and effort, then the assembly line probably does better.

C. A Super-Optimum Solution

The super-optimum solution is to strive for the kind of factory that Japan has pioneered that is highly productive and not dehumanizing because it involves only highly skilled humans in the form of executives and engineers, and nobody on an assembly line except robots. Somebody may be on a console platform watching the robots. He or she may also be watching television. Just like farmers in big harvesters having televisions in their cabs, very different than working with a scythe to harvest wheat.

We can refer to that as highly automated assembly plants. Japan does not even like to use the word factory because it implies something that is belching smoke. They call their automobile manufacturing plants assembly plants. General Motors frequently calls its automobile factories forges, which really sounds like belching smoke. The word assembly though sounds like assembly line, but you can have things being assembled without a line of people turning a bolt like Charlie Chaplin in the dehumanizing movie on the Ford automobile company.

Such a plant is better than a 3.5 score on productivity, maybe even a 5. It is a quality workplace with very few injuries or unhappy employees. The energy source is more likely to be reasonably clean rather than coal-burning. It may even be nuclear energy, although that raises safety issues for people outside the assembly plant rather than inside, or both. The safety of nuclear energy is a separate issue. One could have a highly automated assembly plant that does not use nuclear energy or coal. It could even use solar energy, although that is not so likely with the current solar technology. It probably uses electricity, and if there are any chimneys belching, they are over at the power company, not in the assembly plant.

Conservative in this context does not mean pro-business. It means preserving traditions and old ways of doing things. Likewise, liberal does not mean pro-labor. It means pro-technology, industrialization, rather than non-industrial lifestyles.

This is different from the Africa business development, although related. The Africa problem is basically large business versus small business, rather than factory versus home. A better way to put it that does bring out the distinction is:

1. The India problem is handicrafts versus machines.
2. The Africa problem is small business (regardless whether they are handicrafts or machines) versus big business (regardless whether they are handicrafts or machines). One could conceivably have a big business that employs a lot of people who work with their hands.

There are two different SOS solutions. One involves a technological fix with machines that do not involve assembly line workers, thus one has the productivity of machines without the dehumanizing of an assembly line. The other problem, i.e., the Africa problem involves a sequential SOS where small business leads to big business and is not an end in itself. That requires consciously encouraging small businesses that are not dead-ends, but are likely to be capable of being expanded. It especially means small businesses that manufacture something, rather than small businesses that sell groceries.

D. Finding Other Super-Optimum Solutions

Finding SOS solutions is facilitated by the use of spreadsheet-based decision-aiding software. It allows one to work simultaneously with many goals, alternatives, and relations. That includes missing information and goals that are measured in multiple ways. Such software also allows for what-if analysis to see how the tentative conclusions change as a result of changes in the inputs. Also see Table 3.5 "Simplified Table on Handwork versus Assembly Line in India Clothmaking."

Table 3.5 Simplified Table On Handwork Versus Assembly Line In India Clothmaking

GOALS / ALTERNATIVES	C Productivity	L Quality workplace
C Hand-crafted work	+	-
L Assembly line work	-	+
N Cottage industries with small machines	0	0
SOS OR WIN-WIN Highly automated assembly plant	++	++

SOS solutions are also facilitated by having checklists based on generalizing from previous examples. Such checklists and examples can be found in the growing literature on super-optimizing. That literature includes win-win dispute resolution, growth economics, and non-zero-sum games.[1] For further details, see the chapter on "Super-Optimizing Analysis and Developmental Policy" in Nagel, *Global Policy Studies: International Interaction Toward Improving Public Policy* (St. Martin's Press and Macmillan, 1991), and the chapter on "Improving Public Policy Toward and Within Developing Countries" in Nagel, *Public Administration and Decision-Aiding Software: Improving Procedure and Substance* (Greenwood Press, 1990).

---

[1] For further details on the problem of handcrafted work versus assembly lines in India, see Sanjiv Misra, "India's Textile Policy and the Informal Sectors" in S. Nagel (ed.), *India Development and Public Policy* (1992). Also see Deepak Mazumclar, "The Issue of Small Versus Large in the India Textile Industry" (World Bank Staff Working Papers, 1984) and Sukhamoy Chakravarty, *Development Planning: The Indian Experience* (Oxford University Press, 1987).

Chapter 4

SOCIAL POLICY CONTROVERSIES

I. EDUCATION POLICY

A. Raising Faculty Salaries Without Raising Taxes in China

This example was developed at People's University and Beijing University especially by Professor King Chow and a graduate student named Lu Junwei. The example involves the dispute between the government and university professors in China over faculty salaries.

The professors have been seeking a salary of approximately 300 Yuan for a certain time period. The government has been willing to give at the most 200 Yuan. The object is to come up with a way in which the faculty members could be paid more than 300 Yuan, but where the government would be able to pay even less than 200 Yuan.

The solution developed by Professor Chow, Mr. Lu, and others, is to institute a system of low tuition throughout the Chinese universities while simultaneously increasing the number of eligible students. The money obtained could be used to pay faculty salary increases without having to draw upon the government's limited resources. Provision could be made for low-income students to receive scholarships or loans, especially loans that would be forgiven if the students go into fields of work that are in short supply. The result would be salaries higher than 300 Yuan for faculty, with a possible reduction of the government's contribution to less than 200 Yuan. The result would also be more people receiving college education to the benefit of national productivity which in turn would bring in increased national income and more government revenue. These various relations are summarized in Table 4.1 on "Evaluating Policies Concerning Chinese Faculty Salaries."

TABLE 4.1 EVALUATING POLICIES CONCERNING CHINESE FACULTY SALARIES

Criteria / Alternatives	L goal — Attract faculty	C goal — − Cost of government	L goal — Equity to students	N goal — + Educated population	N goal — + GNP	N goal — Political feasibility	N total (Neutral weights)	L total (Liberal weights)	C total (Conservative weights)
L Alternative Faculty demand	4	2	3	4	4	2	38 (18)	43 (23)*	33 (13)
C Alternative Government offer	2	4	3	2	2	4	34 (18)	35 (19)	33 (17)*
N Alternative Compromise	3	3	3	3	3	3	36 (18)	39 (21)	33 (15)
SOS Alternative Tuition and scholarships	5	5	4	5	5	5	58 (28)	62** (32)	54** (24)

NOTES:

1. For those who prefer numbers to words, the faculty demand can be thought of as 300 monetary units, the government offer as only 200 units, and the compromise as 250 units.

2. The super-optimum solution consists of the government paying the faculty 190 monetary units, but the faculty receiving 310 monetary units. The difference comes from establishing a low-tuition system to replace the current non-existent tuition system. The low tuition system would provide for scholarships and other forms of student aid for those students who cannot afford the tuition. The SOS would also allow for larger student enrollment without lowering admission standards.

3. The intermediate totals in parenthesis are based on the first three goals. The totals not in parenthesis are based on all six goals including the indirect effect of the alternatives.

This is an example of a super-optimum solution where everyone comes out ahead. The low faculty salaries have also been a point of antagonism between the government and graduate students who anticipate becoming professors, especially when sellers of orange pop and cucumbers can make more in a few days than a university faculty member makes in a month. Also see Table 4.2 "Simplified Table on Evaluating Policies Concerning Chinese Faculty Salaries."

Table 4.2 Simplified Table On Evaluating Policies Concerning Chinese Faculty Salaries

GOALS / ALTERNATIVES	C 1. Decrease cost of government.	L 1. Attract faculty. 2. Equity to students.
C Government offer.	+	-
L Faculty demand.	-	+
N Compromise.	0	0
SOS OR WIN-WIN Tuition and scholarships.	++	++

The Chinese faculty salaries problem thus illustrates such broader aspects of public policy evaluation as:

1. Having a third-party benefactor is a useful way of arriving at super-optimum solutions, but the third-party benefactor does not have to be the government. That is especially so when the government is one of the two main parties. In this context, the third-party benefactor was in effect the students paying tuition.

2. The importance of considering the side effects of an SOS solution on the gross national product. Those side effects include (1) the multiplier effect which occurs as a result of increased income causing increased income for numerous other people via a chain of spending, (2) the compound interest effect which occurs from an increase in the base to which next year's growth rates are applied similar to getting compound interest on interest, (3) the inter-generational effect as a result of improving parental role models, (4) the taxpaying feedback effect due to the increased GNP generating more tax money and subsidy money even if the tax rate is constant or lowered, (5) the export surplus effect which occurs via a productivity surplus that is available for export to obtain new capital goods and technologies which further increase productivity, and (6) the welfare reduction effect whereby the prosperity of an increased GNP means less of a burden on the government to provide for unemployment compensation, public aid, public housing, food stamps, Medicaid, and other forms of welfare. These six points emphasize the upward-spiral benefits of investing in human resources and new technologies for increasing the gross national product.

3. The importance of considering equity and not just effectiveness and efficiency in evaluating alternative public policies. It is ironic that equity may be more considered in an affluent capitalistic society than in a hard-pressed Marxist society, even though Marxism in theory is supposed to be more sensitive to the spread of benefits and costs across economic classes and ethnic groups.

B. Tri-Lingualism in Philippine Education

The alternatives are:

1. Only English in the schools.
2. Only Filipino in the schools.
3. Both English and Filipino.
4. The SOS emphasis is not what language is used, but what the substance is that is covered. The emphasis is placed on substance that is relevant to national productivity. See Table 4.3 "Trilingualism in Philippine Education."

All of these alternatives involve the local dialect as well. There is no way of avoiding that, which is where the third language comes in. As far as ideological orientation is concerned, speaking only English is associated with conservative elites, and speaking only Filipino has a left-wing nationalism to it. Retaining both is the neutral compromise. The SOS can be referred to as the language of productivity, although with English in order to enable Filipinos to have access to the literature of the world that relates to productivity. It does not make any sense to talk about the language of productivity. That is the subject matter. It is not a separate language.

The *goals* were:

1. Access to the world's literature. That is not an especially good way to put it. It sounds like access to Mark Twain, Edgar Allen Poe, etc. We are talking about textbook literature. Just say access to the world's books.
2. National unity. The first goal is basically conservative. The second goal is basically liberal, although not necessarily so. That is where we developed three groups, A, B, and C, at least with regard to the alternatives.

The A, B, C alternatives are:

1. The A alternative is only English. That is endorsed by conservative business people who would like to have more access to international trade. It is also endorsed by liberal intellectuals who would like to receive more Fulbright grants and contribute to the literature in their fields.
2. The B position of only Filipino appeals to cultural conservatives, but also to left-wing nationalists.

TABLE 4.3 TRILINGUALISM IN PHILIPPINE EDUCATION

ALTERNATIVES / CRITERIA	Access to World's Books	Unity	TOTALS			
			A Access Wgt = 3 Unity Wgt = 2	B Access Wgt = 1 Unity Wgt = 3	C Access Wgt = 1 Unity Wgt = 1	D Access Wgt = 3 Unity Wgt = 3
A Only English	5	4	23	17	9	27
B Only Filipino	2	4	14	14	6	18
C Only Local Dialect	1	1	5	4	2	6
D Both English and Filipino	4	4	20	16	8	24
SOS Both on Productivity	5	5	25	20	10	30

3. The bilingual position comes out neutral, regardless whether the first and second positions are considered liberal or conservative.

As for *scoring the relations*, it looks like in order to replicate what occurred in the course we need a third position which says only the local dialect. If we call that position C, then it comes out to be a totally dominated position since it provides the worst with regard to access to the world's books and the worst with regard to national unity.

In this context, combining English and Filipino should give the benefits of both. It does not, though, because it detracts from learning English in comparison with teaching only in English. It also detracts from national unity, since both English and Filipino are presented by people who speak only a local dialect, which is a very substantial percentage.

The big problem at the University of the Philippines was deciding how to *assign weights* if the alternatives were not clearly conservative or liberal.

1. The people who take the A position would give a high weight to access to the world's books, and maybe only a weight of 2 to national unity.
2. The people who advocate speaking only Filipino are giving a low weight to access and a high weight to unity.
3. The people who advocate teaching in the local dialect are giving a low weight to access and a low weight to unity. They are giving a high weight to localism. That alternative may not have been used. It is one thing to say that there is no way of stamping out local dialects. It is another thing to say that the national educational system should encourage local dialects by arranging for books and teachers in every local dialect. We may eliminate that alternative as not being reasonable. What we may wind up with, though, is a fairly traditional analysis in terms of the liberal and conservative nature of the alternatives and goals.
4. We could say that the bilingual group is group C, and that it is placing a high weight on both access and unity. It could be referred to as the D group, rather than the neutral group.

With these weights, we can calculate four different *total columns*. The way things are now set up, we are operating independently of liberal and conservative concepts. The example thus serves the useful methodological purpose of how that can be done. Table 4.3 helps clarify and summarize the alternatives, goals, relations, and weights. Also see Table 4.4 "Simplified Table on Trilingualism in Philippine Education."

Table 4.4 Simplified Table on Trilingualism in Philippine Education

GOALS ⟍ ALTERNATIVES	C Access to worlds' books.	L Unity.
C Only English.	+	-
L Only Filipino.	-	+
N Both English and Filipino.	0	0
SOS OR WIN-WIN Both on productivity.	++	++

II. CHECHNYA SOCIAL POLICY

A. Secession of Chechnya from RSFSR

Table 4.5 which follows shows the application of SOS analysis to the problem of the proposed secession of Chechnya from the Russian Soviet Federated Socialist Republic. This application was developed in collaboration with Edward Ojiganoff, the Head of the Policy Analysis Division of the Supreme Soviet of the RSFSR. The Chechnya problem is partly analogous to the proposed secession of Croatia from Yugoslavia or the secession of any ethnic region from a larger country of which it has been a part.

The alternatives in the RSFSR-Chechnya situation are:

1. Deny independence to Chechnya. This can be considered the relatively conservative position because it seeks to conserve the country, state, or political unit as it is.
2. Grant independence to Chechnya. This can be considered the relatively liberal position because it is more tolerant of dissident attitudes.
3. Retain Chechnya as a sub-unit within the RSFSR but grant Chechnya more autonomy than it presently has. This can be considered the relatively neutral position.

TABLE 4.5 SECESSION OF CHECHNYA FROM THE RSFSR

CRITERIA ALTERNATIVES	C GOAL Greater Russia & High RSFSR GNP	L GOAL Chechnya Independence & High Chechnyan GNP	N TOTAL (Neutral Weights)	C TOTAL (Conservative Weights)	L TOTAL (Liberal Weights)
C ALTERNATIVE Deny Independence	3	1	4	7*	5
L ALTERNATIVE Grant Independence	1	3	4	5	7*
N ALTERNATIVE More Autonomy	2	2	4	6	6
S ALTERNATIVE Economic Union	≥2.5	≥2.5		≥7.5**	≥7.5**

The goals in the Chechnya situation are:

1. A key conservative goal is to favor greater Russia and seek a high national income for Russia.
2. A key liberal goal is to help Chechnya, including a high national income for Chechnya.
3. More goals can be added later and possibly more alternatives. For the sake of simplicity, however, we will begin with three basic alternatives and two basic goals.

The relations between those three alternatives and those two goals can be expressed in terms of a 1 to 3 scale. In that context, a 3 means that the alternative is relatively conducive to the goal. A 2 means neither conducive nor adverse. A 1 means relatively adverse or negative to the goal. Relations can also sometimes be expressed in dollars, miles, 1-10 scales, question marks, or other units.

Denying independence to Chechnya is perceived as being at least a mildly positive 3 on the goal of favoring greater Russia. Granting independence to Chechnya is perceived as being at least a mildly negative 2 on favoring greater Russia. More autonomy is in between, with a neutral score of 2. On the other hand granting independence to Chechnya is scored a 3 on the goal of helping Chechnya. Denying independence is scored a 1 on helping Chechnya. More autonomy is in between on that goal, with a neutral score of 2. Those perceptions and scores are likely to be approximately held by both conservatives and liberals in this context.

There are three total scores that can be generated from this data. The total scores are neutral, conservative, or liberal, depending on the relative importance of the two goals. If the two goals are considered to be of equal importance, then the neutral totals are 4 for each of the alternatives. If the conservative goal is considered more important than the liberal goal, we can count the conservative column twice. That results in totals of a 7 for denying independence (3 + 3 + 1), a 5 for granting independence (1 + 1 + 3), and a 6 for more autonomy (2 + 2 + 2). Thus with conservative weights for the goals, the conservative alternative wins on the conservative totals.

Likewise, if the liberal goal is considered more important, we can count the liberal column twice. That results in totals of a 5 for denying independence (3 + 1 + 1), a 7 for granting independence (1 + 3 + 3), and a 6 for more autonomy (2 + 2 + 2). Thus with liberal weights for the goals, the liberal alternative wins on the liberal totals. The single star shows the winning alternative on each total column before the SOS alternative or super-optimum solution is taken into consideration.

The object is to find a super-optimum solution which will simultaneously (1) win on the conservative totals over the conservative alternative and (2) win on the liberal totals over the liberal alternative. That means being better than both the conservative best and the liberal best using their own goals and weights to judge what is best. In terms of the simple scoring system, such a solution needs to score positively or better than a neutral 2 on a 1-3 scale on both goals. That also means going above traditional tradeoff reasoning. The conservative alternative usually does well on the conservative goal, but not so well on the liberal goal. The liberal alternative usually does well on the liberal goal, but not so well on the conservative goal. The SOS alternative does at least mildly well on both goals.

Doing well on both goals does not require being a winner on each separate goal. It means being a winner on each of the two main totals. Those totals involve using conservative weights and liberal weights respectively. If the suggested SOS alternative receives a 2.5 on each goal. then it will receive a 7.5 on the conservative total (2.5 + 2.5 + 2.5). That is higher than the 7 received by the conservative alternative. Likewise, the suggested SOS alternative will receive at least a 7.5 on the liberal total (2.5 + 2.5 + 2.5). Also see Table 4.6 "Simplified Table on Secession of Chechnya."

Developing an SOS alternative which has those characteristics requires a knowledge of the subject matter and some imagination. Finding such an alternative can be aided by the checklists which have been developed from previous case studies as described in Section VI-C of Chapter 1 above in the section entitled "Generating Super-Optimum Solutions." That section briefly describes eight useful approaches. Finding such alternatives can also be facilitated by decision-aiding software which makes use of multi-criteria decision analysis with a spreadsheet base. Such software is described in the book by Nagel on *Decision-Aiding Software: Skills, Obstacles, and Applications* (Macmillan, 1991).

Table 4.6 Simplified Table on Secession of Chechnya

GOALS ⟍ ALTERNATIVES	C 1. Greater Russia. 2. High RSFSR GNP.	L 1. Chechnya independence. 2. High Chechnya GNP
C Deny independence.	+	-
L Grant independence.	-	+
N More autonomy.	0	0
SOS OR WIN-WIN Economic union.	++	++

A proposed SOS solution to the problem of Chechnya seceding from the RSFSR is to allow Chechnya its independence but as part of an economic union with the RSFSR and possibly other autonomous regions within the RSFSR and other neighboring political units. This is analogous to the RSFSR, the Ukraine, and Byelorussia withdrawing from the USSR and forming an economic union or commonwealth. Such an economic union can benefit both the RSFSR and Chechnya by facilitating a profitable interchange of goods, capital, workers, and ideas. It can later lead to developing a more meaningful division of labor than previously existed with the possibility of well-targeted subsidies and incentives from the economic union to make the division of labor even more successful.

An alternative SOS might be to retain Chechnya within the RSFSR, but seek to achieve the benefits of an economic union through immediate subsidies. Such an alternative may not be economically feasible from the perspective of the presently hard-pressed RSFSR. It may also not be politically feasible from the perspective of the independence-seeking Chechens. To be a meaningful SOS requires satisfying the following five criteria:

1. The SOS must win on the conservative totals.
2. It must also win on the liberal totals.
3. It must win by a safe enough margin for the SOS to retain first place regardless of reasonable changes in scoring the relations between the alternatives and goals or in indicating the relative weights of the goals.
4. The SOS must be politically feasible so that it is capable of being adopted.

5. The SOS must be administratively feasible so that it is capable of being successfully implemented, including backed by sufficient funding.

III. YUGOSLAVIA AND SUPER-OPTIMUM DISPUTE RESOLUTION

This section is designed to discuss some aspects of applying super-optimum dispute resolution to Yugoslavia. Its preparation was suggested as part of the presentation of super-optimizing dispute resolution at the invitation of the Russian Academy of Sciences and Moscow State University on December 17-20 1991.[1]

A. Super-Optimizing in General

Super-optimizing involves resolving disputes like the dispute between Serbia and Croatia in such a way that all major sides and viewpoints can come out ahead of their best initial expectations simultaneously. It has been applied to various public policy disputes and litigation disputes. The basic ideas are described in Section VI of Chapter 1 above. Super-optimum can be applied to such problems as resolving the disputes between:

1. Factions in the People's Republic of China who favor a strict policy of one child per family versus factions who favor more reproductive freedom.
2. Factions in various developing countries who favor the retention of large land holdings versus factions who favor the break up and distribution of large land holdings.
3. Factions in the Soviet Union who favor retention of as much government ownership and operation as possible versus factions who favor as much privatization of ownership and operation as possible.
4. Factions in the United States who favor relatively high minimum wages for workers versus factions who favor relatively low minimum wages for workers.

The basic steps or elements in super-optimizing analysis are:

1. Indicating the alternatives that are in dispute.
2. Indicating the goals which each side is seeking to achieve.
3. Indicating how each alternative relates to each goal.
4. Drawing a tentative conclusion as to which alternative is best in light of the various goals and relations.

---

[1] For background on Yugoslavia, see "The Policy Process in Eastern Europe: Nationalities in Yugoslavia" in Stephen White et al., *Communist and Postcommunist Political Systems: An Introduction* (St. Martin's, 1990) and "Socialist Federated Republic of Yugoslavia" in Richard Staar, *Communist Regimes in Eastern Europe* (Hoover Institution, 1988).

5. Doing a what-if analysis to see how the tentative conclusion or conclusions change if there are changes made in the alternatives, goals, the relative weight or importance of the goals, and the relations between alternatives and goals.[2]

B. Super-Optimizing Applied to Secession and Unity in Yugoslavia

The SOS analysis can be applied to Yugoslavia. Some special points worth noting include the following:

1. Each republic and autonomous province of Yugoslavia could become a separate sovereign nation or at least each republic could They would each have a population and a national income that would be within a low to middle range among members of the United Nations.
2. They would be joined together in an economic union of six republics. This would be analogous to the joining of the seven former republics of the Soviet Union or the approximately ten nations in the European Economic Community. The so-called Eurasian Economic Union is more applicable since the members were formerly part of one country
3. The new economic union could be referred to by such names as the Yugoslavia Economic Union, or the South Europe Economic Union. The latter would allow for other South European countries to join, such as Greece. An alternative would be to have a Yugoslavia Economic Union consisting of the six Yugoslavian republics, but having the Yugoslavia Economic Union later join in a larger economic union covering South Europe or possibly Central Europe.
4. The Yugoslavia Economic Union could add to its unity by having a constitutional monarchy as part of the union. The precedent for doing so is the former British Commonwealth. It is now the Commonwealth of Nations, but many of those nations still have a relation to Queen Elizabeth which gives them more unity, tradition, and stability than they otherwise would have.
5. In the case of Yugoslavia. a democratic constitutional monarchy could serve a unifying peacemaking role. Crown Prince Alexander does evoke a favorable response from among many Serbs, Croats, Slovenes, and other Yugoslavian ethnic groups. He probably evokes a more favorable response than the Yugoslavian national or federal presidency or other governmental institutions.
6. As of 1991, there are increasing case studies and experiences regarding the benefits and processes related to forming an economic union. Such unions are becoming increasingly important in such places as Western Europe, the Soviet Union, and the trilateral pact among the United States, Canada, and Mexico.

---

[2] For background on super-optimum dispute resolution, see S. Nagel and M. Mills, *Multi-Criteria Methods for Alternative Dispute Resolution* (Quorum Books, 1990); and S. Nagel and P. Zuckerman, *Resolving International Disputes through Win-Win or SOS Solutions* (SOS Group, 1991).

7. Moving ahead toward establishing such a union may make more sense in ending the civil war in Yugoslavia than trying to achieve a fasting cease fire or a military solution.

8. The economic union can at first emphasize the unhindered exchange of goods, people, capital, and ideas across all the boundaries of the former republics. It can also emphasize equality of opportunity for all ethnic groups in terms of equal treatment regardless of origins in matters of rights that relate to politics, criminal justice, education, employment, housing, and consumer rights.

9. The economic union can later develop appropriate divisions of labor in terms of making the best use of the land, labor, and capital of each former republic. That kind of division or specialization can be facilitated by well-targeted subsidies and incentives available to the economic union.

10. Such an economic union is a super-optimum solution since it enables conservative nationalists and separatists to achieve more national identity and stature than they otherwise would have. At the same time, it satisfies the liberal emphasis on quality of life in terms of jobs and consumer goods.

11. It makes more sense than each country going off on its own without the benefits of the economic interaction associated with an economic union. It likewise makes more sense than forcing nations into a regional government above the member nations, or even a world government.

12. Some of these ideas are summarized in Table 6.9 entitled "International Economic Communities and Super-Optimum Solutions" in Chapter 6, Section VII on International Economic Communities.

13. These are general ideas with lots of potential for Yugoslavia in terms of peace, prosperity, and political reform. These ideas need to be further developed in collaboration with policy-makers, political scientists, economists, and other relevant people mainly in Yugoslavia.

14. The most appropriate next step may be to engage quickly but meaningfully in that kind of collaboration in order to develop and implement a worthwhile plan for creating a Yugoslavia Economic Union of six sovereign states. It could possibly include a constitutional monarchy as a peacemaking unifying force. It could bring together Serbs, Croats, Slovenes, Muslims, Albanians, Macedonians, Montenegrins, and other Yugoslavians.

C. Memo to the Crown Princess Katherine of Yugoslavia

Dear Katherine:
I have received information by phone and fax from Yugoslavia regarding the situation and what might be done about it. The following analysis is based on information and recommendations from highly knowledgeable political and social scientists in Yugoslavia.

1. Some Relevant Facts

1. *The Crown Prince is being increasingly viewed in Croatia and Slovenia as a Prince of Serbia. His association with Serbia is not an insurmountable obstacle if he were doing more to indicate that he is the Crown Prince of Yugoslavia, including Croatia and Slovenia.*

2. *The Crown Prince is being increasingly viewed in Serbia as being associated with the Serbian opposition and not the Serbian government. That is also not an insurmountable obstacle if he were doing something to indicate that he is actively trying to promote the well-being of both Serbian factions, as well as all the Yugoslavian republics.*

3. *Whatever aid the royal family is providing to Croatian refugees and Serbian refugees is virtually unknown in Croatia and Serbia. The attempt to maintain a low profile to promote an image of neutrality has promoted an image of doing nothing in a time when action is needed, including political action more than charitable action.*

4. *Each day in which nothing is done means more killing and more hatred between Croats and Serbs. That hatred has probably already made impossible a unitary state or even a confederation, but not necessarily an economic union.*

5. *The idea of an economic union to promote mutually profitable economic interaction among former emotional enemies has a number of precedents. They include France and Germany in the Western European Economic Community, and Armenia and Azerbaijan in the Eastern European Economic Commonwealth.*

2. Some Relevant Recommendations

1. *The UN and the EEC are tainted as peace-makers in view of their perceived bias in favor of Croatia and Slovenia, especially the EEC. Croatia's seeking the Blue Helmets of the UN also taints the neutrality of the UN.*

2. *The United States and Russia have maintained neutrality partly because of domestic politics and domestic economics, respectively. But their perceived neutrality can be helpful in peace-making and follow-up activities.*

3. *The key recommendation is to get the United States and Russia to call a conference like the one they called in Madrid to resolve serious problems between Israel and its Arab neighbors.*

4. *Neither the US nor Russia wants to get involved unless requested to do so in a way that would result in their being embarrassed if they rejected the request.*

5. *For reasons that relate to loss of face and the difficulties involved in reaching the right people, such a request is not likely to come from the President of Croatia or the President of Serbia, separately or together.*
6. *Such a request could come from the Crown Prince and Princess of Yugoslavia. It would have to be public to be effective. A private request can be too easily rejected. It would also have to be public in order to do the Yugoslavian royal family any good.*
7. *The public request should be directed to President George Bush of the United States and President Boris Yeltsin of Russia.*
8. *The exact wording of the request is not so complicated or lengthy. It should, however, be developed jointly with such people as Paul Wolfowitz of the U.S. State Department, Edward Ojiganoff of the Russian Policy Analysis Division, and relevant people in Yugoslavia.*
9. *For further details, phone me at 217-352-7700. I would be willing to participate in the wording of the request and in the follow-up activities designed to implement the peace-making efforts and the establishment of a mutually profitable economic union.*

3. A Call for Positive Action

I look forward to receiving your favorable reaction to these general ideas, and especially to seeing them successfully implemented. The opportunity to save Yugoslavia is rapidly disappearing through acts of omission by those who could be doing something about it. There should be no more waiting for a deteriorating situation to change by itself.

D. Points and Counterpoints with Professor Danica Hafner

The following memo summarizes the six points made by Professor Danica Fink Hafner of the Political Science Department at the University of Ljubljana in Slovenia.

Her six points are in response to the previous section of this material which is entitled "Super-Optimizing Applied to Succession and Unity in Yugoslavia." Her overall reaction is skepticism toward the idea of an economic union among the independent states that were formerly republics within Yugoslavia. Following each of her points is a brief counter-argument as to why the idea is meaningful.

1. Firstly, Yugoslavia is usually treated as one society divided into six political entities. Contrary to this approach, some sociological and politological studies in the last decade, which were provided among all ex-Yugoslav republics, showed that we can talk about six specific societies. It became obvious that there were (are) major differences among these republics in some very important aspects like social structure, type of political culture, characteristics of the ruling elite, etc. According to these empirical data, there were (are) significant differences between republics even when we focus our attention to only one social group (for example, to youth). Some other significant

differences among these republics are obvious from statistical data on the most important indicators of economic vitality, etc.

The counter-argument: All those things are somewhat irrelevant to the idea that people mutually profit from economic interaction. No matter how much the antagonism might be with regard to any of those groups, they are quite capable of buying and selling goods from each other, investing capital in each other, working for each other, and exchanging ideas wherever it is likely to be mutually economically profitable.

2. Secondly, the super-optimum solution analysis was based on the presumption that the political will of different republics is formed on the basis of rational political thinking. There are a lot of indicators showing this is not the case. This assumption is especially true in the case of relations between Serbia and Croatia, and in the case of the political role which the Yugoslav army plays.

The counter-argument: SOS analysis does not ask Croatian guerrillas or Serbian irregulars to do the analysis. All they need to do is recognize the benefits of the results. It is like the light-bulb analogy. One does not need to be able to invent a light bulb in order to know how to turn one on.

3. Thirdly, the proposed SOS solution has already been offered in the form of a proposal to build up a kind of "clack" confederation of six republics (Slovenia put forward the proposal at the end of 1990 and in Spring 1991) but negotiations among the presidents of the (ex)Yugoslav republics were not successful, and the proposal was turned down. I do not see any new indicators of change in political will in favor of that proposal--just the contrary.

The counter: The economic union is not a confederation idea. A confederation is a political entity in which the sub-units become part of a country or a nation-state. It differs from a unitary form of government in that under a unitary form of government the main power is in the central government to allocate to the states. Under a confederate form, the main power is in the states to allocate to the central government. Under a federal form the power tends to be in a constitution which allocates some to the central government and some to the states. All three are forms of intergovernmental relations within a single country. They are not ways of relating independent countries to each other.

4. Fourthly, experiences about reliability of practicing of agreements in the field of monetary politics during the last years, and especially during the year 1990, were extremely negative. Printing new money by Serbs, in opposition to agreed policy on the federal level, is a very strong negative variable in analyzing the possibility of building up a new kind of economic integration which would include integration in the field of monetary policy.

The counter: That refers to (in the Yugoslavian context) printing new money to deal with economic problems. That is obviously inflationary. It decreases the buying power of the dollar. It has an adverse effect on the economy in the so-called long run, which may come very quickly. Its adverse effect is due to the fact that many people may not have increases in their salaries and wages in order to be able to deal with the inflation of prices. The modern way of dealing with the problem is in the short run to index all prices including the price of labor so that everything goes up simultaneously. The longer term solution is well-placed subsidies and tax breaks designed to increase the productivity of the economy so that one does not have a lot of money chasing a small supply of goods, but instead has a big supply of goods with the supply possibly being big enough to even bring prices down in order to get the goods sold.

5. Fifthly, an objective analysis, made in Slovenia by economists, is an argument for the result of your analysis but negative public opinion does not agree with it. For example, the latest data on the public opinion in Slovenia (December 1991) has shown that about 60% of Slovenes agree with the developing of economic contacts with ex-Yugoslav republics in the same way and on the same level of integration as with the neighboring countries (Italy, Austria, Hungary), or as with other foreign countries. It seems that we can also say similarly about the dominant opinion inside the Slovene political elite at the moment.

The counter: There is nothing incompatible with Yugoslavia being an economic community that joins other economic communities. They are not mutually exclusive ideas.

6. Sixthly, it is impossible to ignore the experiences and economic, political, and psychological consequences of the war in Slovenia and Croatia, the identification of the Yugoslav army with Serbs and Montenegrins, etc. I am not sure that the analogy of the "Yugoslav case" with the "case of the Soviet Union" is entirely correct. One of the most important arguments for that assumption is a different position and characteristics of the biggest republic in the frame of the Soviet Union and of ex-Yugoslavia. That argument is especially indicated by the fact that the Russian republic is the actor and the initiator of political transformation--just contrary to the role of the Serbian public, which tries to hold back the necessary political changes.

The counter: Serbia is just one of the six republics. The other five together plus support they are receiving from the UN and the EEC means that Serbia cannot dictate what is going to happen. The Serbian army is inefficient and disorganized. It has not been paid, or is being paid with money that does not have much value. There have been mass desertions by non-Serbs from the Yugoslav army. Young draftees are refusing to move up to the front. Both Danica and Ivan Grdesic tend to view Serbia as more powerful in reaching a solution than the events described in the New York Times seem to indicate, including the fact that the makeshift Croatian army is moving back the Serbian army in a number of places. The result is likely to be that all sides are at least mildly receptive to some kind of external encouraged solution. If Serbia thought it was going to win within the next few days or weeks, it would not be receptive. All reports seem to indicate that Serbia is not going to win within the next few months or years, if ever. The war is largely stalemated, although that does not mean that it is a non-killing war like World War I in the period of the trench warfare. It is a mobile killing war in which a lot of civilians are also being killed even though nobody is gaining the upper hand.

IV. LAND REFORM IN CENTRAL AMERICA:
EXAMPLES OF UNDESIRABLE POLICY ANALYSIS

We would not want people to get the wrong impression that improved policy analysis means replacing only socialistic ideology with more effective methods or super-optimizing methods. The policy problem of land reform in the Philippines is a good example of where capitalistic ideology as a matter of hindsight tends to look a bit foolish. That is in comparison to more systematic policy analysis which concerns itself more with watching for side effects and unintended consequences. We are not advocating a compromise between socialism and capitalism. We are advocating a *super-optimum solution* that achieves socialistic goals better than socialistic policy analysis can, and that simultaneously achieves capitalistic goals better than capitalistic policy analysis can.

One of the most interesting aspects of the Philippine land reform experience has been the many mistakes (or one might call them learning experiences) that have been made by well-intentioned agricultural experts who may have been overly focussed in their expertise. This can be contrasted with policy analysts who have a more generalist perspective. One should try to see how different policy problems and proposed solutions can interface with each other. Some alternatives have a domino effect where the unintended consequences become devastating to what otherwise looks like a meaningful approach to increased agricultural productivity.

Four examples were given by the people associated with agrarian reform in the Philippines. The first example involves informing farmers as to how they can double their crops through better seeds, pesticides, herbicides, fertilizer, and machinery, but not providing for any increased storage facilities to put the doubled crop. The result was that much of the increased productivity rotted in the fields.

The second example involved informing farmers how they could arrange for as many as four crops per year, instead of one crop per year through special seeds that have a three-month season. The crops thus go from being put into the ground to being ready to harvest every three months. The farmers, however, were not informed as to how a one-person farm could plow, weed, and harvest four times a year and still be able to attend fiestas.

The third example involved supplying the farmers with new pesticides that kill all the crop-damaging insects and weeds, but also the frogs and fish that live on the farms that the farmers like to eat. After the frogs and fish are killed, the pesticides and herbicides are withdrawn realizing that the farmers did not want to kill the frogs and fish. The result is the farmers now have no frogs, no fish, and the insects are back. The thing to do might have been to continue with the pesticides, but give the farmers food stamps to buy frogs and fish from the local markets. The economy would then be better off because the increased farm productivity would more than offset the cost of the frog and fish stamps.

The fourth example involved showing the farmers how they can grow more efficiently with a tractor than with an ox. Such a demonstration may, however, fail to recognize that tractors do not make good fertilizer. The demonstration may also fail to recognize that if you give one farmer a tractor and not other farmers in the area a tractor, then the other farmers come to borrow that farmer's tractor, especially his relatives. That farmer then has no tractor, no ox, and no fertilizer. The correct solution might have been to give the tractor to the whole community collectively to share, the way American farmers share grain elevators or Russian farmers share tractors at machine tractor stations.

The idea of one tractor per Philippine farmer is American individualistic-capitalism gone berserk, contrary to the realities of farming in the Philippines and other developing countries, or even developed countries. Every farmer in Champaign County, Illinois does not have a combine, and they do not feel deprived. They find it more efficient to hire a combine company just as every American does not own a U-Haul trailer or a Greyhound bus, although they use them. Farmers want to own their own land at least in most developing countries. There are many American farmers, however, who own no land, but who farm for land owners. They often make a lot of money getting paid to do it with their equipment. Wanting to own one's own land does not mean one wants to own a combine. The land is used almost all year long if you are a farmer. The combine gets used for one week, and it is recognized as wasteful to have to store it, depreciate it, and make payments on it on a year-round basis. There is a need for combining individualistic land ownership with collectivistic sharing and renting.

In a socialistic society like China, the combination of individualism and collectivism might take the form of retaining government ownership of the land and renting land to farmers who will personally and productively work the land. The rent they pay serves as a substitute for property taxes. The rent can be lowered to provide a strings-attached subsidy to encourage the adoption of new herbicides, pesticides, farm machinery, hybrid seeds, and other biotechnology. There is also the possibility of non-renewal of the one-year lease or other term if the farmer-renter violates reasonable rules relating to the environment, workplace safety, labor relations, consumer relations, employment discrimination, or other socially-desired standards of behavior. Non-renewal of the lease is much easier to implement than traditional regulatory measures which emphasize fines, injunctions, litigation, threats, and other more difficult to impose negative sanctions. This would also avoid buying land for windfall gains or tax-avoidance purposes, as contrasted to land for food production.

A. Alternatives, Goals, and Relations as Inputs

If we are talking about 100 units of land, the typical conservative alternative tends to advocate retaining most of the ownership of the land in the hands of the traditional landed aristocracy. The typical liberal approach tends to advocate turning most of the ownership of the land over to landless peasants to farm. The typical neutral or compromise approach is something in between, although not necessarily exactly a 50-50 split of the 100 units, as shown in Table 4-7 "Land Reform in Developing Countries.".

TABLE 4.7 LAND REFORM IN DEVELOPING COUNTRIES

CRITERIA ALTERNATIVES	C Goal Productivity	L Goal Equity	N Total Neutral Weights	L Total Liberal Weights	C Total Conservative Weights
C Alternative Retain land (0 units)	4	1	10	7	13*
L Alternative Divide land (100 units)	1	4	10	13*	7
N Alternative Compromise (50 units)	2.5	2.5	10	10	10
S Alternative 1. Buy the land 2. Lots of land 3. Co-op action	4.5	4.5	18	18**	18**

Notes:

1. The SOS package combines an individualistic desire to own land with collectivistic action to make more efficient use of shared technology and ideas.

2. It is not an SOS package to give farmers technology or ideas out of the context in which the farmers operate, such as:
    (1) Ideas on fertilizer for increasing acreage yields, without providing increased storage capability,
    (2) Ideas on seeds for multiple crops within a given time period, without providing increased labor or technology to handle the increased work,
    (3) Ideas on pesticides and herbicides for destroying insects and weeds which may also destroy frogs, fish, and other edible animals, without providing for food stamps or other replacements, and
    (4) Ideas on farm machinery without providing for a fertilizer replacement and a system of sharing the machines if there are not enough machines for every farmer in the area to own one.

The two key goals in the controversy tend to be agricultural productivity and a more equalitarian or equitable distribution of land ownership. The conservative alternative (by allowing for economies of scale that are associated with large land holdings) is more productive, but less equitable. The liberal alternative (of widespread land distribution) is less productive, but more equitable. The neutral compromise is somewhere between those relation scores, just as it is somewhere between the conservative and liberal distribution alternatives.

With those relation scores, we logically have the result mentioned above, where the conservative alternative wins with the conservative weights, and the liberal alternative wins with the liberal weights. We are also likely to get the classic compromise, which is everybody's second best alternative or worse. The "or worse" means that sometimes liberals accept the compromise when the conservative alternative actually does better on the liberal weights, or the conservatives accept the compromise when the liberal alternative actually does better on the conservative weights. Each side may accept the compromise even though it is the third best alternative to them, because they do not want to give in to the other side. That is not the case with Table 4.7, but it does sometimes occur in the psychology of public policy-making. Also see Table 4.8 "Simplified Table on Land Reform."

Table 4.8 Simplified Table on Land Reform

GOALS ALTERNATIVES	C Productivity	L Equity
C 1. Retain land (0 units)	+	-
L 1. Divide land (100 units)	-	+
N 1. Comprise (50 units)	0	0
SOS OR WIN-WIN 1. Buy the land 2. Lots of land 3. Co-op action	++	++

B. Finding a Super-Optimum Package of Policies

The super-optimum alternative seems to involve three key elements. The first is that the land needs to be bought from the present landowners, rather than confiscated. If the owners are threatened with confiscation, one possible reaction is to establish death squads, to bring in American military power, or to do other especially nasty things that may easily cost more than the cost of buying the land. The United States probably could have saved a fortune in military and other expenditures on Nicaragua, El Salvador, and Guatemala over the last 10 or 20 years by simply using a fraction of the money spent to buy land from the owners to give to the peasants. The landowners would have probably also saved themselves money by paying a substantial portion of the taxes needed to buy the land.

The second element is that lots of land needs to be involved. It cannot be a token program. The landless peasants in developing countries are no longer as passive as they once were. They cannot be easily bought off with trinkets, pie-in-the-sky religion, patronizing aristocrats, and other relatively worthless bribes or distractions. They have demonstrated a willingness to fight and die for land in pre-communist China, in Central America, and in other developing countries, including the Philippines.

The third element is the need for using modern technologies in a cooperative way to overcome the divisive effect of distributing the land in relatively small parcels to the landless peasants. Here is where the policy-makers can learn from both capitalistic American farmers and communistic Russian farmers. American farmers are highly individualistic, but they recognize that it makes no sense for each of them to own their own grain elevators, combines, and other big equipment which they can own collectively through producer cooperatives. In the Soviet Union, agricultural efficiency has been promoted through machine tractor stations where farmers can collectively share tractors which they can not afford to own separately. This is true regardless whether the individual farmers are associated with collective farms or private plots. Cooperative activities also involve the equivalent of county agents who help bring farmers together to learn about the latest seeds, herbicides, pesticides, fertilizers, and other useful knowledge. Cooperative action can also include credit unions and drawing upon collective taxes for well-placed subsidies to encourage the diffusion of useful innovations.

With that combination of SOS elements, one can have agricultural productivity and equity simultaneously. Doing so enables that combination of elements to be a strong winner on both the liberal totals and the conservative totals. Appropriate timing may also be required in the sense of moving fast to implement these kinds of ideas. The longer the delay, the more difficult such an SOS solution becomes. The reason is that the liberal left may acquire such a negative attitude toward the conservative right that the liberal left would consider buying the land to be a surrender to evil people. Likewise, the conservative right may acquire such a negative attitude toward the peasant guerrillas that they can see no respectable solution other than extermination of what they consider to be terrorists.

Chapter 5

POLITICAL POLICY CONTROVERSIES

I. VOTING RIGHTS IN SOUTH AFRICA

A. Alternatives, Goals, and Relations

The conservative *alternative* to voting rights in South Africa has been to deny blacks the right to vote. The extreme left-wing alternative of some of the Pan-Africans has been to deny whites the right to vote. Or even to expel them from the country, meaning deny that they have any right to even live in South Africa. The middling position is everybody has one person, one vote, although that could be considered a left-wing position since the blacks would dominate.

The black *goal* is basically for blacks to be better off. The white goal is not necessarily for whites to be better off than they presently are, but to at least not be much worse off.

The conservative position and the more extreme left-wing position would *result* in a kind of super-malimum position where both blacks and whites would be worse off.

1. The only way the conservatives could succeed in keeping blacks from having the right to vote any longer would be through a system of repression even greater than they have attempted in the past. The country would be in a state of continuous guerrilla warfare with no security from being bombed or assassinated. There would be no foreign business, or not much that would want to locate there. Much domestic business would leave.

2. If the extreme blacks had their way and all the whites were driven out, the result would be somewhat similar in that there would be a lack of foreign investment. Much domestic business would leave voluntarily or involuntarily.

B. Developing an SOS

The *object* is to develop a system in which none of those bad things happen, meaning:

1. Foreign investment does not shy away from South Africa, but substantially increases.
2. Businesses within South Africa stay there and even expand to hire more people and make for more job opportunities.
3. Violence ends as contrasted to merely being temporarily suspended as the situation is now, waiting to see what will happen.

The compromise position is not really one person, one vote. That is the non-extreme left-wing position. The *extreme* left-wing position is no voting rights to whites at all. At least at the present time, the conservative position is not to deny blacks access to jobs, public accommodations, schools, etc. The conservative position is to wipe out all apartheid and all segregation except for voting rights. The *extreme conservative* position is to preserve all apartheid and segregation.

The *compromise* position is one person, one vote but some kind of guarantee that whites will not be outvoted in spite of the fact that they have so much fewer people. The proposed devices are:

1. Partition the country into states like the United States, especially as of the 13 states. Every state no matter how small gets two senators. There would be basically four states in South Africa, namely the Cape provinces, Natal, Transvaal, and the Orange Free State. The first two would be black, the last two could be dominated by Afrikaans. There would be not eight senators. Maybe each state would have five senators so there would be 20 senators. But the blacks could not run the Senate any more than the north could run the U.S. Senate. The white states would have the power to prevent even ordinary legislation from being passed, but especially any legislation that requires a 2/3 vote like the approval of treaties or appointments and any amendments to the constitution would require a 3/4 vote.
2. Everything that has been proposed is exactly what was adopted in the United States in the constitution. There would be separation of powers, federalism, judicial review. Everything designed to enable a minority of states to be able to prevent the majority from exercising the power that its numbers have. They would have an electoral college in which the president would be chosen on the basis of how many senators each state has which would have nothing to do with how many people they have since every state would have the same number of senators. They would have a supreme court that would have the power to declare unconstitutional legislation that interferes with property rights, state's rights, all of which would be code words for white people's rights.

3. It is ironic that those who want to preserve white power in South Africa choose as their model the American constitution, including the Bill of Rights. They are all of a sudden very much in favor of minority rights because they are the minority. Here the word minority means numerical minority, not lacking in power.

A super-optimum solution would have to involve something that would be the equivalent of an internal economic union. It would have to involve a system whereby white business interests would have an environment in which they could prosper, and blacks would have job opportunities accompanied by merit criteria, affirmative action with preferences for people who cannot satisfy a minimum competence level. It basically means going directly to what it is that each side wants to achieve by way of in-creased voting power and concentrating on how to more than guarantee that regard-less of the voting rights. It means elevating certain economic rights to a higher status than the status of federalism, separation of powers, and those other constitutional issues.

C. Relevant SOS Reasoning

The key way out is to emphasize both blacks and whites being much better of economically as a result of SOS thinking. That is, political power is directed toward economic well-being for each group.

A key thing is to get away from stability toward continuous economic growth. Also to get into responsiveness in regard to upgrading skills rather than forming a new government. Making those rights meaningful includes a right to sue but also the establishment of appropriate institutions like a ministry of international trade and industry. I had overemphasized the right to sue, although that can be part of it.

There are three responses or questions or types of questions that can be asked of revolutionary South African blacks:

1. What is going to happen to the whites? That is an implicitly racist question that shows rather biased sensitivity to what is going to happen to the whites but not what is going to happen to the blacks who may be in bad shape as a result of white flight, loss of investment, and other socio-economic disruptions.
2. How to get whites and blacks to make concessions? That is the traditional compromise position, which is better than civil war.
3. The SOS question is how to enable both blacks and whites to be better off than their best expectations. The SOS dispute resolution activity is one that we are getting increasingly involved with. See Tables 5.1 and 5.2.

Table 5.1. Voting Rights in South Africa

	C GOAL Whites Well Off C=3 N=2 L=1	L GOAL Blacks Well Off C=1 N=2 L=3	N TOTAL (Neutral Weights)	L TOTAL (Liberal Weights)	C TOTAL (Conservative Weights)
C Alternative Only Whites Vote	4?	2	12	10	14*
L Alternative Only Blacks Vote or Maj. Rule w/o Minority Safeguards	2	4?	12	14*	10
N_1 Alternative (Bill of Rights) (See Note 1)	3	3	12	12	12
N_2 Alternative (U.S. Const.) (See Note 2)	3	3	12	12	12
S Alternative (Economic Rights) (See Note 3)	> 3.5	> 3.5	> 14	> 14	> 14

NOTES:
1. Neutral Alternative 1 is minority safeguards like (1) free speech, (2) equal treatment, and (3) due process.
2. Neutral Alternative 2 is minority safeguards like (1) senate, (2) electoral college, and (3) special majorities to pass, amend.
3. The SOS Alternative includes (1) economic growth, (2) upgraded skills combined with Neutral Alternative 1 and some Neutral Alternative 2.

Table 5.2 Simplified Table On Voting In South Africa

GOALS ⟍ ALTERNATIVES	C Whites well off.	L Blacks well off.
C 1. Only whites vote.	+	-
L 1. Only blacks vote. 2. Majority rule without minority safeguards.	-	+
N 1. Bill of rights: Free speech, equal treatment, due process. 2. U.S. Constitution: Senate, electoral college, special majorities to pass, amend.	0	0
SOS OR WIN-WIN 1. Economic rights: Economic growth, upgraded skills combined with neutral alternatives.	++	++

II. CHINESE POLICY STUDIES

Public policy studies can be defined as the study of the nature, causes, and effects of alternative ways that governments deal with social problems. The most interesting aspects of policy studies relate to evaluating the effects of alternatives, although knowing the nature and causes of the alternatives is important to understanding why some policies are adopted more readily than others

Evaluating alternative public policies in a systematic way involves processing a set of societal goals to be achieved, policy alternatives available for achieving them, and relations between goals and alternatives in order to arrive at or explain the best alternative, combination, allocation, or predictive decision rule. That conception of policy studies is geographically independent since it applies across countries. It is also independent of subject matters since it is applicable to economic, social, technology. political, or legal policy problems.

A. Pre-Modern Developments

The development of policy studies in China has been well ahead of the rest of the world in some ways but behind in others. When much of the western world was in the process of converting from warlike Teutonic tribes into nation-states, China had a well-developed and studied governmental system. One could find insights into governmental decision-making in the writings of Confucius and others before Aristotle, Machiavelli, and other western governmental scholars.

However, when the western world was undergoing its middle-class American and French revolutions, China was still associated with authoritarian dynastic government. When the western world was undergoing industrial change and social reform through relatively peaceful means associated with the New Deal and western European socialist parties, China and the Soviet Union were undergoing revolutionary ideological change.

B. Ideology, Technocracy, and Synthesis

As of the 1970's, the People's Republic of China was seeking to resolve public policy problems largely by consulting the ideological writings of Karl Marx, Mao Zedong, and their interpreters. As of the 1980's, government agencies in China, were seeking to become more professional by way of the introduction of personnel, management, financial administration, and other bureaucratic ides from the West, some of which are actually a throwback to Confucius bureaucracy.

Thus ideology became offset by technocracy. What we were seeing may fit the classic Hegelian and Marxist dialectic of thesis, antithesis, and synthesis. Ideology represented the prevailing thesis in the 1970's, whereby population control might be analyzed by reading Marx and Mao. Technocracy represented the antithesis in the 1980's, whereby population control might be analyzed by reading biological literature.

The 1990's may represent a super-optimum synthesis of the best, not the worst of both possible worlds. It may draw upon the idea of having goal-oriented values from the ideological thesis, as contrasted to rejecting values as being unscientific or not objective. Values and goals may be quite objective in the sense, of being provable means to higher goals, or in the sense of proving that certain alternatives are more capable of achieving the goals than others.

The 1990's may also draw on the idea of empirical proof based on observable consequences, rather than ideological labels of socialism or capitalism. It is empirical proof that also makes sense in terms of deductive consistency with what else is known about the world, rather than mindless technical number crunching without thinking about how the results might fit common sense. Being technical does not necessarily mean being effective in getting the job done efficiently and equitably, which is what should really count in governmental decision making.

C. Moving to a Super-Optimum Synthesis (SOS)

The kind of synthesis to which SOS refers is a synthesis of goals to be achieved (the ideological element) and systematic methods for determining which alternative or alternatives most achieve these goals (the technical element). The true dialectic is dynamic not only in the sense that a thesis leads to an antithesis, which leads to a higher-level synthesis, but also in the sense that a synthesis does not stagnate but becomes a subsequent thesis to be resynthesized by a new antithesis into a still higher level of analysis. There may be policy evaluation methods that are even more effective, efficient, and equitable.

Those are the methods that are hinted at in various places in this book where super-optimum solutions are explicitly or implicitly mentioned. Such solutions enable conservatives, liberals, and other viewpoints to all come out ahead of their best initial expectations simultaneously. Traditional optimizing involves finding the best alternative or alternatives in a set. SOS analysis involves finding an alternative that is better than what conservatives previously considered the best and simultaneously better than what liberals previously considered the best, using both conservative and liberal values.

D. Some Conclusions

One point that was made by the participants in the seminars where materials like these were presented in China was that developing countries like China cannot afford the luxury of super-optimum solutions. Instead, they should perhaps be satisfied with something substantially less than super-optimum. That point sometimes implied that super-optimizing was too complicated except for people trained in computer science, mathematics, statistical analysis, operations research, and other sophisticated methodologies.

After the presentations, however, the consensus generally was that those methodologies are largely irrelevant. They can sometimes even be harmful if they cause paralysis or an overemphasis on unnecessary measurement and data. The prerequisites for super-optimizing analysis are basically to have (1) some knowledge of the key facts relevant to the problem, (2) an awareness of such political concepts as conservative and liberal, (3) an understanding of such decisional concepts as goals, alternatives, relations, tentative conclusions, and what-if analysis, and (4) some creativity in developing appropriate super-optimum solutions. This kind of creativity is made easier by having the first three of the four prerequisites. It is also made easier by having access to case studies like the ones previously discussed, so that one can learn from the experiences of other groups or individuals in trying to develop related super-optimum solutions.

The point about not being able to afford the luxury of super-optimum solutions may be the opposite of empirical and normative reality. The United States and other developed countries have less need for super-optimum solutions than developing countries do. The United States can probably go for a whole generation without developing any innovative ideas or coming close to solving any of its policy problems. If that happened, the United

States would still have a high quality of life because it has such a well-developed cushion to fall back on. Developing countries, on the other hand, cannot afford to be satisfied with merely getting by. Doing so will put them further behind relative to other countries that are advancing rapidly, including countries that were formerly developing countries: Japan, Korea, Hong Kong, and Singapore.

In that context, super-optimum solutions are like free speech. Sometimes people in developing countries say they cannot afford free speech because it is too divisive. After they become more developed, then they can allow opposition parties and not have one-party systems with presidents for life. The reality is that they especially need to have free speech to stimulate creative ideas for solving their policy problems. Those problems are much more in need of solutions than the policy problems of well-developed countries.

A concrete example is the polio problem in Malawi. The country does not need Jonas Salk to invent a polio vaccine. The vaccine has already been invented. The country just needs to use it. Malawi does not use the vaccine adequately, not because it lacks the technology of having bottles of vaccine to pour into paper cups to give to the children to drink the vaccine but because Malawi happens to have a one-party state with a president for life who thinks that only doctors can give out vaccines, partly because he happens to be a doctor himself. People who speak out against that nonsense may find themselves in jail or worse. The problem is thus a free speech problem, not a technology problem.

On a higher level, the problem is an SOS problem. Polio could be greatly reduced or eliminated in Malawi by explaining to the headman in each village how to pour the vaccine from the bottles into the paper cups and how to have the children drink the vaccine. Doing so would probably mean the end of polio in Malawi, as it has meant the end of polio in the United States. President Hastings Banda could get the credit for having been responsible for ending what has been a horrible disease since the dawn of history in Central Africa. That should please the liberals, who are interested in better public health care. It should please the conservative president, who wants to be admired. More important, if this situation can be used for establishing a precedent about the importance of free speech in stimulating better public health care and better resolutions of other public policy problems, then the impact might extend to numerous ways in which the quality of life could be improved in the developing country of Malawi.

This is not an isolated example. Numerous examples have already been given in the previous case studies, and more examples could be given. What is needed are more applications of the basic ideas mentioned above, including the prerequisites for super-optimizing analysis. It is hoped that this chapter and the book of which it is a part will help stimulate those applications toward achieving super-optimum solutions to the public policy problems of developing and developed countries.

III. CHINESE PUBLIC ADMINISTRATION

Public administration can be defined as the study of the methods for improving and understanding how governmental programs are implemented, especially in terms of personnel, financing, and accountability.

One purpose of this section is to analyze systematically some of the recent developments in Chinese public administration. "Systematically" in this context refers to using a super-optimizing perspective for understanding and improving Chinese public administration. Such a perspective emphasizes methods whereby all major sides and viewpoints in a dispute or dilemma can come out ahead of their best initial expectations simultaneously.

Table 5.3 analyzes the problems of ideology versus technocracy in Chinese public administration. From the establishment of the People's Republic of China to about 1980, the emphasis was on ideology in evaluating alternative ways of implementing governmental programs. That meant referring to Mao, Marx, Lenin, or interpreters of them. The results in personnel management were to emphasize hiring on the basis of ideological loyalty and Communist party enthusiasm, rather than an emphasis on technical skills. As of about 1980, an increased emphasis was placed on knowledge of economics in administering a business program, engineering and physics in administering an energy program, or other substantive fields for other programs.

In terms of Table 1, the basic alternatives are ideology, technocracy, or a compromise between the two. Equity was the key goal of those supporting the ideology alternative. It was, however, often a lip-service goal when personal status was the real goal. Efficiency and effectiveness was the key goal of those supporting the technocracy alternative. It likewise was also often a lip-service goal with personal status being the real goal of those with technocratic skills.

In the late 1980's, more emphasis began to be placed on public administration as it is known in the United States, Western Europe, and countries with American-trained professors and practitioners in public administration. That emphasis recognizes the importance of equity in governmental programs including postal systems, elementary schools, urban transportation, and other governmental services that take a loss in providing services to the poor and many other people in order to provide more equal access and equity. That emphasis also recognizes the importance of efficiency and effectiveness as manifested in the use of decision analysis, operations research, management science, and other such generalist techniques to supplement the substantive expertise which goes with business administration, engineering, physics, and other relevant substantive specialties.

Striving for both equity and efficiency simultaneously is associated with the super-optimizing idea of enabling the Group 1 ideologists and the Group 2 technocrats to both come out ahead of their best initial expectations. With regard to personnel, an enlightened public administration approach talks in terms of equality of opportunity to apply for and meet the entrance requirements in governmental positions. At the same time, there is a setting of high quality standards to promote efficiency and effectiveness. Likewise, the broadened perspective on public finance may emphasize the income taxes to provide equity, but sales and other consumption taxes as an efficient way of collecting large sums of money.

TABLE 5.3 IDEOLOGY VERSUS TECHNOCRACY IN CHINESE PUBLIC ADMINISTRATION

CRITERIA / ALTERNATIVES	C Goal Equity C=3 L=1	L Goal Efficiency & Effectiveness C=1 L=3	N Total (Neutral Weights)	C Total (Conservative Weights)	L Total (Liberal Weights)
C Alternative Ideology	4	2	12	14*	10
L Alternative Technocratic	2	4	12	10	14*
N Alternative Compromise	3	3	12	12	12
S Alternative Both Simultaneously	5	5	20	20**	20**

NOTES:

1. Symbols in these tables include: C = Conservative, L = Liberal, N = Neutral, S = Super-Optimum, #1 = Group 1, and #2 = Group 2.

2. The 1-5 scores showing relations between alternatives and goals have the following meanings: 5 = the alternative is highly conducive to the goal, 4 = mildly conducive, 3 = neither conducive nor adverse, 2 = mildly adverse, 1 = highly adverse.

3. The 1-3 scores showing the relative weights or multipliers for each goal have the following meanings: 3 = this goals has relatively high importance to a certain ideological group, 2 = relatively middling importance, and 1 = relatively low but positive importance.

4. A single asterisk shows the winning alternative on this column before considering the SOS alternative. A double asterisk shows the alternative that simultaneously does better than the conservative alternative, on the conservative totals, and better than the liberal alternative on the liberal totals.

TABLE 5.4 SOS APPLIED TO PESONNEL RECRUITMENT

CRITERIA ALTERNATIVES	G1 Goal Decent Wages G1 = 3, G2 = 1	G2 Goal -Overpayment G1 = 1, G2 = 3	N Total Neutral weights	G1 Total X G1 Weights	G2 Total Y G2 Weights
G1 Alternative Applicant A	4	2	12	14*	10
G2 Alternative Applicant B	2	4	12	10	14*
N Alternative Applicant C	3	3	12	12	12
S Alternative Hire "A" with OJT	5	4	18	19**	17**

Table 5.5 Rewarding Performance

GOALS ALTERNATIVES	C Elitism.	L Democratic sharing.
C Reward high performance.	+	-
L Winners of lower goals.	-	+
N Reward moderate performance.	0	0
SOS OR WIN-WIN Ask for higher performance but with subsidized facilitators.	++	++

This more general analysis is applied in Tables 5.4 and 5.5 to personnel administration and in Tables 5.6 and 5.7 to financial management. Table 5.4 involves a classic personnel recruitment problem. Applicant A does well on the first goal, but not so well on the second goal, although above a minimum threshold. Applicant B does well on the second goal, but not so well on the first goal. The traditional recruitment might be to hire Applicant C who is a compromise in the sense of doing in the middle on both goals. The super-optimizing alternative might be to hire Applicant A in order to obtain the benefits of his or her high quality on goal 1, but provide on-the-job training to raise Applicant A on goal 2 to a level close to that of Applicant B. Applicant B would he hired with OJT training if the nature of the skills were such that it is easier to train on goal 1 than on goal 2.

Table 5.5 deals with the conflict between the conservative or elitist desire to reward especially high performance versus the liberal or democratic desire to have lots of people rewarded even if lower goals are achieved. The SOS alternative might be to ask for even higher performance than the conservatives or elitists are advocating, but provide subsidized facilitators to enable more people to achieve those high performance levels. The subsidized facilitators might especially include skills-upgrading and the introduction of new technologies.

Table 5.6 Tax Sources

GOALS / ALTERNATIVES	C Stimulating investment	L Ability to pay
C Sales tax	+	-
L Income tax	-	+
N Other or both	0	0
SOS OR WIN-WIN Decrease tax rates, but increase taxes with lots of well-placed subsidies	++	++

Table 5.6 provides an SOS approach to tax sources. The conservative alternative emphasizes sales taxes. They disproportionately bear on the poor rather than the rich. The liberal alternative emphasizes income taxes. They disproportionately bear on the rich rather than the poor. A compromise is to have both, but with neither kind of tax bringing

in as much revenue as might be needed. The super-optimizing perspective seeks to increase both kinds of taxes in order to have sufficient funding for needed governmental programs. The key element in a super-optimizing perspective seeks to increase both kinds of taxes in order to have sufficient funding for needed governmental programs. The key element in a super-optimizing approach (as reflected in the policies of both Ronald Reagan and Bill Clinton) is to try to have a system of well-placed subsidies and incentives so that total taxes will increase even if the tax rate comes down.

Table 5.7 Current Deficit

GOALS ⟍ ALTERNATIVES	C Defense and investment	L Domestic and consumption
C 1. Decrease domestic spending 2. Increase taxes poor	+	-
L 1. Decrease defense spending 2. Increase taxes rich	-	+
N 1. Decrease both spend 2. Increase taxes both	0	0
SOS OR WIN-WIN 1. Increase spending 2. Decrease taxes	++	++

Table 5.7 involves the important financial management problem of dealing with annual deficits in large and possibly increasing national debt. All these personnel and financial problems cut across both developing and industrialized countries. The conservative alternative to dealing with the deficit tends to decrease domestic spending and increase consumption taxes. The liberal alternative tends to decrease defense spending and increase income taxes. The neutral alternative is eclectic, doing a little of everything.

The super-optimizing alternative seeks to increase rather than reduce spending, but spending to upgrade skills and introduce new technologies that will pay off in terms of a larger gross national product. The SOS approach may also use selective tax reductions with strings attached in order to reward productivity-increasing activities. This kind of perspective is especially associated with the public finance aspects of the industrial policy of Japan and West Germany. It is also associated with newly industrializing countries or dragons of the Far East including South Korea, Taiwan, Hong Kong, Thailand, and South China.

IV. KOREAN UNIFICATION

A. An SOS Approach to Unification (By Cheol Oh)

1. An Overview

Historically, Korea has experienced an incomparably longer period of unity than of division. However, for thirty-five years between 1910 and 1945, Korea had to go through the disgrace of being a colony of Japan. Furthermore, the Korean peninsula was forcefully divided under the unfortunate Yalta agreement before even the liberation at the end of World War II was fully enjoyed by the Korean people. For the next forty-five years between 1945 and 1990, the Koreas have thus remained a divided nation and, subsequently, become collective victims of the cold and hot wars between super powers in the international politics. In short, the Korean peninsula has not seen a united and independent nation for the last eighty years (1910-1990). The Korean people are, however, determined to put an end at this unhappy chapter in their history before this century fades away and to welcome the twenty-first century as a proud and unified nation (Lee, 1989). When we add to the relatively long, historical continuity of Korea, the striking ethnic homogeneity of the Korean people, and their common language, the imperative of unification becomes more compelling.

Until recently, the best known formula for Korean unification was one offered by North Korea. Inasmuch as North Korea has tried to make the best political advantage out of the trap-laden proposal, it at the same time calls for a response from Seoul with a comprehensive and workable plan. Pyongyang's proposal for a "Democratic Confederal Republic of Koryo" basically consists of a dual structure of government with a unified governing body, that is, two separate governments for North and South governed by a unified body. Its counterpart, Seoul, until recently advocated "a national unity, democratic government" formula, which called for cooperation and exchanges in nonpolitical areas between the two Koreas to facilitate ultimate reunification. In doing so, South Korea wanted to establish a ground for mutual understanding and trust as a preliminary step toward unification. In his speech to the National Assembly on September 11, 1989, President Roh Tae Woo of the Sixth Republic of Korea introduced a new comprehensive formula for achieving national unification, officially known as the "Korean National Community Unification Formula." In so doing, Mr. Roh fulfilled a pledge he made in the National Assembly in October 1988 to present a "feasible and reasonable formula for peacefully unifying our homeland" (Koh, 1989).

In short, there are now two different formulas for Korean unification, each of which represents the position of South and North on unification. With these available policy alternatives in mind, a practical and significant question would then be: Which formula is the proper method for unification? Or is there any other alternative way of approaching Korean unification? This paper is about examining Korean unification from a new policy analysis perspective, that is, the super optimum solution (SOS). This paper is organized in terms of (1) presenting some of background knowledge related to Korean unification (i.e., conditions for unification and key features of two formulas) and (2) applying the SOS to the Korean case and discussing how conflict resolution in a divided country, i.e., Korean unification can be better approached in terms of the SOS.

2. Emerging Conditions for Unification

Why is a need for discussing and/or embodying Korean unification escalated at this time? Or in particular, why is a new comprehensive formula by Seoul introduced at this time? Several important factors (reasons), that is, external and internal, may be offered to explain the reopening of talks between South and North about unification and the need of South Korea for a new comprehensive formula. A few broad trends are currently discernible in the international and domestic political arenas.

First, is the ending of the Cold War as exemplified by the emerging "New World Order." That is, the collapse of the Soviet Union has definitely sped up the end of ideology-laden confrontations between so called democratic and communist countries. Gorbachev's "New Thinking" prompted major Soviet initiatives in the areas of arms control, East-West relations, and wide ranging economic and political reforms within the Soviet Union as well as reforms within Eastern Europe (i.e., the independence of the Baltic nations). As a result, the wind of reform has blown over the Korean peninsula. During the period of global confrontation, the USSR and USA were looking at Korea in the light of their own military and political rivalry. However, with the end of global confrontation (at least in terms of military rivalry) and the fall of one of the superpowers (i.e., the Soviet Union), the Korean peninsula is no more a hot place for the battle of ideology and seeking interests of superpowers.

Secondly, the economic and social achievements of South Korea, the success of the 1988 Seoul Olympics, and the improving democratization of South Korean society--all these factors have strengthened self-confidence and self-esteem of the Korean people and changed the political image of South Korea. That is, Seoul has showed the world that South Korea is a promising economic and political partner for cooperation whom one needs (Mikheev, 1989). Especially, with its success in "northern policy," which is the main new aspect of Seoul's friendly gesture toward socialist countries, Seoul has gained increasing prominence in the international arena. President Roh, for example, declared his will to stop the confrontation with Pyongyang, to help North Korea in its international activities, and to develop close relations with socialist countries including the USSR and China (Mikheev, 1989). Since October 1988, South Korean firms were partially allowed to develop direct trade with North Korean counterparts. In January 1989, Hyundai Group founder Mr. Chung Ju Young visited Pyongyang to discuss joint-ventures and various other projects, i.e., Soviet-DPRK-ROK economic cooperation in the Soviet Far East. And the most recent case is the visit of Mr. Kim Woo Jung, President of Daewoo Group, to Pyongyang and talk with Kim Il Sung about economic cooperation between two parts in January 1992. In South Korea there is a widespread belief that it is necessary to help the "brothers" in North Korea to improve their standards of living. GNP per capita in the South ($4,000 as of 1989) is eight times that in the North ($500), and the DPRK needs tons of foreign money to vitalize its dipping economy. Seoul already announced that it was ready to help Pyongyang revitalize its economy and pay North's debt to the Western countries of $1.5 billion. Moreover, recent agreement between South and North signed by prime ministers (i.e., denuclearization on the Korean peninsula and increasing contacts) has moved both sides closer to the possibility of the summit meeting between President Roh Tae Woo and Kim Il Sung.

Thirdly, there have been some changes on the side of North Korea. That is, some improvement can be seen in Pyongyang's harsh relations with Tokyo and Washington. That is, anti-North sanctions were lifted by Japan, and the USA at the end of 1988. Political contacts between the Workers Party of North Korea and Japanese Socialist Party become more active, and the media have reported on contacts, even informal, between North Korean officials and Japanese authorities. Likewise, North Korean-American non-officials contacts started (Mikheev, 1989). In addition, there has appeared a new emphasis of Pyongyang on adjusting to the rapidly changing international situation and, subsequently, improving its inter-Korean activity. Unlike previous years, since 1988 North Korean leaders began to speak about signs of a gradual relaxation of international tensions in the world, and about ties between South and North and the relaxation of tension on the Korean peninsula (i.e., in 1991 South and North Korea became members of the U.N.).

3. Key Features of Two Formulas for Korean Unification

Here, we will present a brief sketch about key features of unification formulas offered by each side. The difficulty of the Korean settlement is to a large extent the result of the prevailing atmosphere of mutual distrust and misunderstanding. The main point of disagreement is the proper method for unification. There are officially two formulas for unification. The "Democratic Confederal Republic of Koryo" by North Korea is basically a political solution to Korean unification. The basic premise of the North formula is that two governments of South and North keep their autonomous jurisdiction and socioeconomic systems under the governing of a unified body. Pyongyang's formula, however, sees only the end-product of a unified Korea without elaborating on how it would be achieved. Contacts and cooperation between South and North are considered to be not preconditions for unification but rather the consequence of political decisions (Han, 1989). Pyongyang's confederal formula is problematic in the sense that it is a part of the communist united front strategy intended to take advantage of the pluralistic nature of the South Korean polity (Han, 1989). As preconditions for its implementation, North Korea's formula calls for the signing of a peace agreement between North Korea and the United States (not South Korea) and the withdrawal of foreign troops from Korea (i.e., the U.S. forces). Pyongyang's formula is also unrealistic and/or illogical because it is implicitly based on some degree of trust and cooperation that do not exist at present between two parts and are themselves, according to the formula, the end product of political integration.

By contrast, the new South Korean proposal, known as "the Korean National Community Unification Formula," is a functional/incremental solution to unification. It is based on the premise that the reuniting of the people will precede the restoration of a politically united state. In other words, a new aspect of South Korea's formula is to set an interim stage toward unification during which both sides will recognize each other and seek co-existence and co-prosperity, regardless of the existence of different political systems. (Lee, 1989). And moving through this interim stage, both sides are expected to finally establish a political integration of the national community. Therefore, both South and North under the "Korean Commonwealth" would be sovereign states; yet, the relationship between them will not be an international relation but a special relation under an interim arrangement (Lee, 1989). In short, the "Korean Commonwealth" is intended to promote the reunification of the Korean people. And, the formula envisages the eventual establishment of a "unified democratic republic (political integration)," preceded by the adoption and promulgation of a unified constitution (Koh, 1989). Seoul's plan has some distinct features. One of them is that the new formula has accommodated some elements of the North Korean proposal on unification. For example, All the organs that will make up the Commonwealth will embody the principle of absolute equality between the two Koreas (for more detail, see Koh, 1989).

It can be in a sense said that from a functional point of view, the step has attributes similar to those of the European Community or the Nordic Council. However, this South Korean plan is in fact a development that would more closely resemble the "German formula," although the Germans themselves never had an explicitly agreed-upon plan such as has been proposed by Seoul (for more detail, see Han, 1989). While "Korean Commonwealth" has been a scenario most preferred by Seoul, it was immediately rejected, indeed feared, by North Korea. In Pyongyang's view, Seoul's proposal is aimed not at achieving unification but at perpetuating the "two Koreas." That is, the Korean Commonwealth is, according to Pyongyang, a recipe for an indefinite extension of confrontation between two states. Pyongyang also contends that when Seoul says it wants a unification of systems, what Seoul really means is a unification in which communism is obliterated. Pyongyang sharply rebukes President Roh for not dealing with the withdrawal of U.S. troops in South Korea and repealing South Korea's national security law. Pyongyang also criticizes Seoul for emulating the German formula and the European Community formula. Accusing Seoul of practicing "flunkeyism (*sadae chuui*), Pyongyang calls on Seoul to accept the proposal for the establishment of the Democratic Confederal Republic of Koryo, which, in its view, symbolizes a genuine Korean approach to Korea's problem (for more detail, see Koh, 1989).

4. The Super-Optimum Solution and Korean Unification

In today's context of North-South Korean relations, when a formula is proposed by one side, it is generally taken by the other as a political propaganda and a measure for subjugation. Indeed, it is not the absence of such a formula that has prevented progress toward unification; rather the lack of sincerity about establishing unification. Under the circumstances that there are already two formulas for unification proposed by each side, and that there are still disagreement and the lack of trust between two sides, the most important question at this point is not whether or not unification is necessary, but what kind of method is more reasonable and feasible. This is, we think, where the SOS can come in. See Table 5.8 on "SOS as Applied to North and South Korea."

Table 5.8 SOS Applied to North and South Korea

GOALS / ALTERNATIVES	C Promote capitalism and well being of Republic of Korea.	L Promote communism and well being of Democratic People's Republic of Korea.
C South Korea prevail.	+	-
L North Korea prevail.	-	+
N Two Koreas.	0	0
SOS OR WIN-WIN Unification.	++	++

In both sides, unifying two Koreas has been taken for granted for a long time, and there are already a number of reasons/justifications for unifying two Koreas offered by a variety of scholars, i.e., historical, international, and domestic reasons. Therefore, the issue is not that unification is the best solution to Korea's problem but that if unification is necessary for whatever reason, how unification can be achieved, that is, what is the most feasible and legitimate way for unifying two Koreas. If the SOS can offer any alternative to the existing unification formulas, i.e., a political and a functional/incremental approach, which both sides can agree to follow and think to get benefit from, then the SOS will contribute to resolving conflicts in divided nations at least theoretically. For example, in the Korean case, North Korea's formula (Democratic Confederal Republic of Koryo) may be an option under L in the SOS, and South Korea's plan (the Korean National Community Unification Formula) can be another option under C in the SOS. Then, what we need to think about is what can be placed under N and under the SOS category. Not to mention to clarify such terms in the scheme of the SOS as liberal, conservative, and neutral in terms of their accuracy in describing Korean situations, the bottom line in this paper is to come up with sensible alternative(s) by use of SOS.

5. SOS

{However, if you want to confine in this paper the application of the SOS to coming up with a justification for unification as an alternative to other options, i.e., conquering by either side, I think the draft is on the track. Then, next things to do may be to clarify terms, to make some justifications for using specific options (i.e., conquering option, this is because while "conquering" may make sense in understanding North Korea's position, i.e., unified front strategy, it makes little sense in figuring out South Korea's position.)}

B. Another SOS Approach

1. Classifying International Disputes

The seven categories of international disputes are:

1. Disputes between sovereign nations.
2. Colonial disputes.
3. Secession disputes.
4. Conflicting nations within a country.
5. Class conflicts in rural areas.
6. Class conflicts in urban areas.
7. Disputes between ideologies.

With regard to the *disputes within countries*, we could subclassify them or add more categories to the basic seven. We are not talking about class conflict disputes or ideological disputes. Those are separate categories. We are not talking about ethnic conflict. The conflict could be secessionist in nature, although not necessarily. There is plenty of race conflict in the United States and other ethnic conflict in which no ethnic group is seeking to withdraw from the U.S. and establish a separate country. The explanation is generally that American ethnic groups are not geographically based, especially the leading minority group of blacks who are now dispersed throughout urban cities in the north and both urban and rural areas in the south.

The *Korean situation* raises some questions with regard to the relevance of the economic union approach to nations that cannot get along with each other. There are a number of analogous situations. The analogy that is most applicable to Korea is East and West Germany where two countries are really a figment of the Cold War and are ethnically one country. Austria is also an example which long ago had its east and west parts united. Thus the solution to Korea and for that matter, Taiwan and mainland China, is political unification and not an economic union.

2. Where an Economic Union is More Applicable

Where an economic union is more applicable than some form of political unification is where the following criteria are present:

1. The economic union is more appropriate where there are separate countries or even provinces within the same country that are ethnically different, like Croats versus Serbs. It is not so applicable where we are talking about East Germans and West Germans, or North Koreans and South Koreans, who all speak the same language and have virtually the same cultural traditions.
2. The economic union is more appropriate where there has been *no recent history of political unification*, as is the case with France and Germany, but is not the case with the Ukraine and Russia which have had a history of political unification going back
3. more than 500 years.
4. The economic union is more appropriate where there is a *lot of trading going on already* between the countries. That means they almost of necessity need to be geographically adjacent. But the English commonwealth is a bit of an economic union and it consists of units that are scattered over the world. Thus, being geographically together is not a prerequisite, although the commonwealth is the only example.
5. One could say that the exceptional situation is where the *political units were former colonies*, and they are held together by a colonial language and some colonial traditions. In that sense there is a bit of an economic union among former French colonies, and Spanish and Portuguese. The U.S. has a kind of economic union with the Philippines and Puerto Rico. That is not really an exceptional situation, it is just another situation that leads to economic union, namely having a set of former colonies that have acquired some kind of dependence or interdependence with a mother country that holds them together in an economic union.

3. None of Those Four Apply to Korea
1. There are no big ethnic differences.
2. The second one with regard to a history of political unification is ambiguous. The way the principle should be stated is that if there is a recent history of having been one country, then the solution may be to be reunited, depending on what split the parts apart. If they were split apart by external forces such as the Cold War, with the U.S. and the Soviet Union dividing up the world after World War II, then the possibility of unification is much more meaningful than if the split involved both sides voluntarily or through violence among themselves going their separate ways. The above tends to rule out the third possibility of remaining totally separate countries. If we are going to reason by analogy, we have no analogies to reason from where that has occurred.
3. There is a lot of trading going on between the two countries. The more trading, the more likely for political unification. The less trading, the more likely for only an economic union. If the trading is zero, like Ecuador and Thailand, even an economic is not appropriate, or virtually zero.
4. The fourth criterion is prior commonality as colonies of the same mother country. That does apply to Korea. For most of its history it has been a colony of either

China or Japan and has only become an independent country in the 20th century. It was remade into a Japanese colony as of about 1935 and did not become independent again until 1945. It became independent around the turn of the century by being taken away from China by Japan, but did not become a Japanese colony until Japan went to war with China and Korea. The colonial background, though, does not mean that Korea is going to become a province of Japan. Japan, unlike France and other colonial countries, does not want to add to its boundaries. This is also unlike the United States which grew by constantly taking over somebody else's territory from France, Spain, Russia, and England. Japan in its militaristic days took over countries but never made them part of Japan. Now in its economic imperialism, it takes over countries in an economic sense. Korea is becoming a competitor with Japan instead of becoming a place where Japan can get raw materials, cheap labor, and sell products. The important thing is that the Chinese colonial influence and the Japanese colonial influence has given both halves of Korea some common background that facilitates unification. If each half had been a colony of a different mother country or only one half had been a colony, they would lack that commonality. Since 1945, North Korea has in effect been a colony of Russia and South Korea has been a colony of the United States. In both cases, the only presence of either mother country was a military presence. In both cases, there was no absorption into either country . Under czarist Russia, North Korea might have been converted into a Russian province. Not so under the Soviet Union. Under McKinley as a president, South Korea might have been converted into an American territory, but likewise, not so in modern times under Truman and subsequent presidents.

The bottom line is that Mr. Oh is very wrong in his analysis of the Korean situation, maybe because he is a Korean and cannot objectively analyze it. As recently as April 29, 1991 in his memo, he says that the situation looks very hopeless and the Chinese analogy is inapplicable. As of December, 1991, the book *South-North Dialogue in Korea*, and articles regularly appearing in the New York Times indicate that unification is definitely moving forward. This is so even though there has been no change in democratization in North Korea, unlike the situation in East Germany. One could argue that North and South Korea can get along better with both of them being dictatorial governments because the dictators in each country can in effect deliver their respective countries into a political union whereas a more responsive democracy might vote against it. That, however, seems irrelevant. If it were put to a referendum in both countries, the people would probably vote in favor of unification as they did in both halves of Germany.

It is important to think in terms of three different categories:

1. A situation where there is international conflict that can be resolved through political unification of both units becoming one country.
2. A situation where both units or all three or more units are not likely to become one country but they can become an economic union.

3. The opposite extreme is where there is no present possibility of even becoming an economic union. The third category has no examples. Every economic union that has been proposed in the world has moved in the direction of being implemented. One could say that there is no economic union between Thailand and Ecuador. The simple explanation is that neither side nor any third parties are proposing that they should form an economic union. Thailand is part of Southeast Asia's economic union and Ecuador is part of the Andes economic union.

4. Not Redundant to the China v. Taiwan Situation
The reasons it is not redundant are:

1. In the China unification, the *dominant portion is a communist dictatorship* with a little capitalistic province being united with the big mainland. In Korean unification, the dominant portion is South Korea which has a much better GNP than North Korea, more population, and more area. It is in a more powerful position to set the terms than the communist dictatorship in the north.
2. In the China situation, a factor that makes things more difficult is that *Taiwan has a long history of wanting to be an independent country*, whereas there is no history of independent countries between North and South Korea until 1945. Thus the Chinese situation is harder to bring unity, not easier, as Mr. Oh implies.
3. The China situation is also harder since *Taiwan is more of a democracy* relative to Beijing than South Korea is to North Korea. Both South Korea and Taiwan are capitalistic, but Taiwan has recently become more democratic. South Korea, though, is more democratic than North Korea. And it is more democratic than China. In other words, there are more political differences between Taiwan and the mainland than there are between North and South Korea, although both have a similar pair of economic differences.
4. The China situation is also easier because mainland China is more concerned with industrialization and trading with the world and wanting to be less isolated than North Korea. A key factor explaining North Korea's willingness is that it can no longer operate in isolation without the Soviet Union's help. It is thus becoming more like mainland China in looking to the west for economic trade. Thus there are some factors that make the Chinese situation more difficult than the Korean to unify, and some that make it less difficult. It adds up to about the same. And both are proceeding in the direction of unification, not economic unions and not independent countries.
5. One key factor that makes the Chinese situation also easier is that the dominant group on Taiwan consists of people who formerly lived on mainland China who would like to return and who identify with the mainland. They are not native Taiwanese. That is not the case in South Korea. South Korea does not consist of a bunch of North Koreans who have fled to South Korea who would like to go back. The nationalist Chinese on Taiwan are ironically a big unifying force even though they are more anti-Communist than the native Taiwanese. This is another illustration of nationalism being more important than economic ideology in

motivating people. The economic ideology enters in not in the sense that the Chinese nationalists are latent communists or are even willing to tolerate communism, but in the sense that they are profit-seeking capitalists and recognize that unification with China can help them make more money than independence. If they do not join with China, then Taiwan is likely to lose out on a great deal of its middlemen trading activities to places like Shanghai, Guangzhou, Hong Kong, and Tianjin. Mainland China no longer needs Taiwan for trading purposes the way it briefly did when there were no economic zones like Guangzhou. Taiwan in effect needs to become an economic zone of the mainland in order to have the prosperity that those places have and not be boycotted by the mainland.

Another difference between the two relates to the fact that Taiwan is worried that because it is so much smaller than the other "half," it will be overwhelmed. Thus, like Hong Kong, it demands special rights that no other provinces have such as the right to maintain its capitalistic system for at least 50 years without interference. Hong Kong has also demanded in return for union with the mainland the right not to have to pay any taxes to the central government for 50 years, which is a big concession on the part of the central government. There may be no province in any country that has a tax exemption like that. South Korea does not demand any such privileges since it dominates the Korean peninsula. The analogy would be for North Korea to demand that it be allowed to retain its communist form of government for 50 years without interference. Nothing has been said about that. The odds are that the communist government will fall in both mainland China and North Korea as soon as present leadership dies off because in both places it has become so personalized.

5. SOS Analysis

The conservative *alternative* would be for South Korea to conquer North Korea and have one dictatorial capitalistic government. The left-wing solution would be to have North Korea conquer South Korea and have one dictatorial communist government. The neutral position might be to keep things as they are with two separate countries that would probably have no trouble getting into the United Nations now that the Cold War is over. Russia would not object to South Korea and the United States would not object to North Korea. The super-optimum solution is unification, not an economic union as previously indicated.

The conservative *goal* is to promote capitalism or at least the well-being of South Korea. The liberal goal is to promote communism or really a kind of Stalinism that is not practiced in other communist countries, although the only communist countries that currently exist are dictatorial communist countries. One can argue that Serbia is an example of a mildly democratic communist country since it does have a multiparty system. But the communists are the dominant party. North Korea, China, and Cuba do not have opposition parties. In no country in East Europe is the communist party the dominant party, but in a number of countries communist individuals and a kind of reform communist party might be in control. That is the case in the Ukraine, for example. The country is being run by the former leaders of the communist party, but they now talk about privatization and allowing other parties. The North Korean Communist Party, though, has not discovered either perestroika or glasnost.

We wind up with the conservative alternative being relatively good in comparison to the left-wing alternative for South Korea, and the left wing alternative being relatively good for North Korea. But the unification solution being in the best interests for both, which is why they are pursuing it. We have to some extent answered above why they are now seeing that unification makes sense when it formerly did not make sense to them. The key answer is that North Korea had been abandoned by the Soviet Union, and South Korea virtually abandoned by the United States.

As of June, 1998, the prospects for unification are better because (1) the new South Korean president has long advocated unification partly because he is not so ideologically opposed to North Korea, and (2) the new North Korean president who is the son of the founder is not so ideologically opposed to South Korea and is in need of economic help.

V. THAILAND PRO-DEMOCRACY CRISIS

A. Part One: Causes

I.   LONG TERM
    A.   Industrialization causing education which causes resistance to being ordered by a dictatorial government.
    B.   History
        1.   1932. Threw off absolute monarchy. Replaced with military controlled government.
        2.   1973. Successful student revolt with much loss of life, 50 to 1,000.
        3.   1976. Restored military until 1988.
        4.   1988. Civilian.
        5.   1991. February Suchinda coup
II. IMMEDIATE CAUSES
    A.   For the Coup
        1.   Choice of deputy defense minister.
        2.   Choice of army commander- in-chief.
        3.   Choice of investigator of assassination plot.
    B.   For the Pro-Democracy Demonstration
        1.   Recent election in March. First prime minister was in drugs.
        2.   Promise of Suchinda not to be prime minister.
        3.   Wipe out corruption, but appointed leading crooks.
        4.   Refusal to call special election.
        5.   Refusal to allow constitutional amendment with grandfather clause.
    C.   For the Killings
        1.   Virtually no use of water cannon, tear gas, or rubber bullets, instead automatic weapons, long clubs, and few shields.

2. Alleges students shoot first, communist takeover, disrupt the monarchy.

3. Isolated head given middle class involvement, the provinces, and some segments of the military.

4. A cornered madman concerned about face.

B. Part Two: Remedies (See Table 5.9)

Table 5.9 Democracy in Thailand

GOALS ALTERNATIVES	C Stability	L Responsiveness
C 1. Retain power. 2. Suppress protest.	+	-
L 1. Resign in favor of elected government.	-	+
N 1. Retain power but make concessions.	0	0
SOS OR WIN-WIN 1. Legal: call special election or amend constitution. 2. External: stimulate democracy by U.S. economic pressure like South Africa. 3. Internal: intervention of monarchy, business, university pressure, etc.	++	++

I. IMMEDIATE
    A. Pressure from Abroad
        1. Total embargo.
        2. Boycott all Thailand products.
        3. Like South Africa.
    B. Pressure from Within
        1. Business buy-off. Business support for opposition Chaulit or Chamlong.
        2. University support for resignation. Restraint is not enough.
        3. More demonstrations, not less.
        4. Military opposition.
        5. Provincial opposition.
        6. Middle class professionals.
        7. Monarchy including king, crown princess, and crown prince.

    8. Mass media.

II. LONG TERM

  A. Withdrawal of U.S. support for the military.

  B. Legal

    1. Constitutional amendment that no prime minister, civil service, or government position while still military.

    2. No prime minister who is not elected.

    3. No military for crowd control.

  C. Socialization into democratic principles of freedom to disagree with government and to be allowed to convert others.

C. Part Three: Predictions Short Term (See Table 5.10)

Table 5.10 Military Versus Civilian Rule

GOALS / ALTERNATIVES	C Respect for military.	L Restraint on military.
C 1. Preserve military power as is.	+	-
L 1. Dissolve the military like Japan, Costa Rica as models.	-	+
N 1. Cut in half.	0	0
SOS OR WIN-WIN 1. Preserve or phase down gradually. 2. civilian rule.	++	++

I. SHORT TERM

    1. Military may refuse to step down. They may stall for time thinking that will lead to loss of interest by demonstrators.

    2. Demonstrators and opposition parties will become impatient and again take to the streets. This time possibly with more anger inspired be perceived support from many or even all major segments of Thai society including some military.

    3. Stubborn vicious military like Suchinda, Kaset, and Issaprong may order troops to stop angry demonstrators. Then killing and maybe counter-killing could be worse than before.

    4. Alternative is face-saving departure with big money to go overseas as in the past.

II. LONG TERM
1. Parties along conservative and liberal lines instead of personalized groups.
2. Maybe judicial enforcement of the constitution.
3. More international, more American, and thus more regard for free speech, due process, and treatment on merit.
4. Contracting out as SOS between private and government ownership and operation.

D. Part Four: Implications from the Thailand Crisis Case Study

1. The problem of civilian versus military government. See the SOS Table 5-10.
2. The problem of stability versus modernization. See the SOS Table 5-11.

Table 5.11 Stability and Modernization

GOALS / ALTERNATIVES	C Minimize disruption.	L Benefits of modernization
C Stability (stagnation).	+	-
L Modernization fast (disruption).	-	+
N Modernization slow.	0	0
SOS OR WIN-WIN Well-placed subsidies and tax breaks emphasized quality.	++	++

3. The causal analysis problem of explaining the success of the pro-democracy demonstrations in Thailand versus their failure in Tiananmen Square.
4. The inconsistencies on the part of American foreign policy that relate to interfering with foreign governments in the Cold War or the drug war, but not even offering non-interfering assistance on behalf of pro-democracy forces.
5. The role of middle class people in bringing about social change, which is a key factor that we have emphasized before as essential to having a stable democracy.
6. The much greater respect for intellectual input in developing countries or, for that matter, almost any countries compared to the United States. That illustrates or relates to saving one of the newspaper headlines which came out I think on Thursday, May 21, and indicated the high regard that people in Thailand have for

what people in the universities are advocating. It may have been in Friday morning's paper in the Bangkok Post. The heading is "Academics Demand a New Government". Behind that is some of the explanation for why Japan is doing so much better than the United States, namely the high regard that Japanese business people like Thai business people have for university professors, especially American university professors.

7. As a kind of quaint aspect of the Thai crisis, that might have some interest to the Serbian royal family. They should observe how the Thai King handled the situation, which is nicely covered in the headline on Thursday's Bangkok Post, that the King tells the factions to work on compromise. Immediately that was the end of the whole violence, demonstrations, and everything immediately resorted back to a peaceful state. It is not because the Thai people are monarchists. It is because the Thai royal family knows how to be a respected royal family. It is also the Thai royal family that is to a considerable extent responsible for the high respect for higher education, with every higher education degree being personally handed to the recipient by a member of the royal family at graduation time and the family having a tree filled with Ph.D.'s, M.D.'s, and the person who is probably most in line for the throne also having a Ph.D. degree.

8. The role of legalistic action is also important in the Thai example in that there is a strong consensus that the situation at its height could be defused through a constitutional amendment, and even now the constitutional amendment idea is important. In other countries, like Latin America, amending the constitution would be considered close to a farce with not much enforcement. In Thailand they take seriously what the constitution provides and want it to specify that no one can be prime minister unless the person is an elected member of Parliament, regardless how many or what percentage of Parliament chooses a non-elected member to be Prime Minister.

9. The situation also illustrates how being stubborn and nonfunctional with regard to face-saving can be self-destructive and interfere with an SOS. The military prime minister could have easily arranged for a special election to get elected and thereby remove the key objection, but refused to do so on the grounds that that would be an admission of wrongdoing. Instead, he lost the whole job and may lose his life as well. Even if he does not lose his life, he is in total disgrace.

10. There may be other implications from that case study which we need to write up. One is the importance of economic boycotts by the United States as bringing about favorable governmental changes. We saw that to some extent already in South Africa and the refusal to do that in China. A big factor that turned the business community against the military prime minister was the boycott that was already in effect contrary to the Bush administration with numerous American importers canceling orders. Not because they were so sympathetic to the pro-democracy movement (though that may have been part of it), but because they explicitly said or implied they did not want to deal with some kind of banana republic military dictatorship. They wanted responsible, businesslike people. The important thing is that kind of economic pressure can definitely change

governmental decision-making. It is ridiculous for the Bush administration to say it would have no effect in China, South Africa, or elsewhere. It simply reflects that the Bush administration does not place a very high priority on changing the overseas governmental decisions in a more pro-democracy direction and that selling a few more widgets is more important.

11. It also has international implications by virtue of setting an important precedent and role model for other developing nations that military dictatorships are not the way to go. That can be the eleventh implication. Thailand is highly regarded in the developing world. It is a newly industrialized country, although the other newly industrialized countries are also getting rid of their military dictators or civilian dictators, or lessening them such as South Korea, Taiwan, and Singapore to some extent.

12. An especially exciting implication of the Thailand-crisis case study is that it generated the concept of an International Dispute Resolution workshop or IDR workshop. Such a workshop builds on the concept of an SOS workshop which the Policy Studies Organization has been conducting since our China workshops of 1989, 1991, and 1992. An SOS workshop is a gathering of professors, practitioners, graduate students, and others to learn about methods for arriving at super-optimum solutions to public policy problems. Such solutions can enable conservatives, liberals, and other major viewpoints to all come out ahead of their best initial expectations simultaneously. An IDR workshop involves the same subject matter as an SOS workshop. It differs from the usual SOS workshop in that at least some of the participants are invited to attend because they are associated with nations, provinces, ethnic groups, or other groups that are in violent conflict with each other. The workshops can last anywhere form a full day (or less) to a week (or longer). The idea is that during that time, the people whose groups are normally in conflict will be simulated to think more about how all sides or viewpoints can come out ahead of their best initial expectations simultaneously.

The IDR workshop that was conducted at Chulalongkorn University during the Thailand crisis was not premeditated. It was supposed to be a SOS workshop. It turned into an IDR workshop because during the conducting of the SOS workshop, the Thailand crisis occurred. Partly by coincidence, the participants in the Thailand SOS-IDR workshop included such people as a colonel in the Bangkok policy force and a pro-democracy former Communist guerrilla teaching in the Public Administration Department. Some of the emotional interaction was defused by virtue of face-to-face contact. Some of it was also defused by virtue of the nature of the subject matter that was being discussed. The subject refers to how all sides to highly emotional disputes can come out ahead of their best initial expectations simultaneously. The Thailand crisis was resolved before anybody participating in the IDR-SOS workshop had an opportunity to communicate any of the ideas to their colleagues in the police system or among the demonstrators. Future IDR-SOS workshops are, however, now being planned that will include people simultaneously from India and Pakistan, and a separate workshop that will include people simultaneously from mainland China and Taiwan.

E. Part Five: Differences and Similarities Between China and Thailand

1. China worse. Beijing has a 90-year-old dictator that people are waiting to die. This causes a restraint on pro-democracy demonstrations. Thailand has or had a 55-year-old military dictator who was in very good health. Nobody suggested waiting for him to die. Many people suggested ways to accelerate his death.

2. Thailand worse. Beijing was actually more restrained in some ways than Thailand. It is a civilian dictatorship, not a military dictatorship. Civilian policy were largely used to deal with the students including unarmed police officers with clubs and some tear gas. They could not use water cannons because Beijing does not have a water system that can get up enough pressure to do any blasting of water at people. The Thailand crowd control consisted of heavily-booted paratroopers with assault weapons including high-powered machine guns and tanks.

3. Both same. A key difference is that Thailand sought to exercise some constraint out of sensitivity to world opinion and the export-import business. Beijing has also been sensitive to that. That is not the key difference.

4. Thailand better. The key difference is that in the past two years the cold war has ended. Many parts of the world have moved greatly toward democratization including East Europe, Africa, Asia, and Latin America. We could give some concrete examples. Thus world opinion and student opinion is less tolerant of dictatorships.

5. The main thing that needs explaining is why the pro-democracy demonstrators succeeded in Thailand and failed in Beijing. The timing may be more important than the place. A further proof of that is that the students failed in 1976 in the same place because the world was not so ready for democracy as it is now including Thailand.

F. Part Six: Examples of the World Moving Toward Greater Democracy

1. In East Europe as of about 1989 at the time of Tianenmen Square, virtually every country had a one-party Communist dictatorship. They now have multi-party systems with more choices for the voters than can be found in the United States.

2. In Africa every founding father is either out or in big trouble. That includes Kenneth Kwanda in Zambia who was voted out. Mr. Mbuto in Zaire and Mr. Moy in Kenya. None of the democracies are in any trouble in Africa. Nigeria is also in trouble. It is run by a military junta. The people in Africa are becoming increasingly educated and unwilling to be told what to do by military or non-military dictators.

3. The military dictators have been thrown out of Argentina, Chile, Brazil, Uruguay, Paraguay, Panama, Nicaragua. There is no place that is an exception with the possibility of Peru. Even Peru represents a move toward greater democracy in the sense of the last presidential election resulting in the first time since the Incas maybe that somebody who was not part of the Spanish elite was elected. In this case it was somebody who wasn't even Hispanic but was Japanese. Although maybe it is possible to be Hispanic Japanese if he is a Peruvian citizen and speaks Spanish.

4. The fourth continent or region is Asia. This is a place where progress is not being made so well, although Thailand is an example of progress in the sense that the military has been thrown out and they are likely to have a civilian government on into the future. In Burma the military has more explicitly taken over than in the past. Japan represents a one-party state as much as ever and sets a bad example. Afghanistan has moved from a Communist dictatorship to what may be a Moslem extremist dictatorship like Iran. That is not quite true. Iran has moved away to a considerable extent from its Moslem extremism. Afghanistan has moved from Communism to more democracy given differences among different Moslem groups than was previously the case. There are rumblings at democracy in Saudi Arabia and Kuwait, although moving very slowly. The Philippines just completed a reasonably democratic election, which is a big improvement over the previous Marcos non-elections. Taiwan has become more democratic. Mainland China has also become more democratic than it was under Mao and the Cultural Revolution. The Tiananmen Square incident was partly a manifestation of pro-democracy desires even though they did not succeed.

5. What it adds up to is the world as a whole is becoming better educated as a result of industrialization and less willing to accept medieval or military dictatorships.

VI. THE PARLIAMENTARY ALTERNATIVE AND NEW CONSTITUTIONAL RIGHTS

This is the fundamental political science dispute between parliamentary and presidential governments, which is applicable to all countries, but especially Latin America like Argentina.

A. The Alternatives

The conservative position is generally to support presidential government because it gives greater stability, which conservatives like. The liberal position is to support parliamentary government largely because it is more responsive and liberals have traditionally been more interested in responsiveness, at least with regard to economic issues (although not necessarily with regard to civil liberties issues). The neutral position is to try to find a middle position, which is not so easy. One can make it easier, to remove the president through impeachment, but that has never been done. One can try to give parliamentary government more stability by saying that it takes a 2/3 vote to bring down the Prime Minister rather than a mere majority vote, but that has never been done. One can have a presidential government with short terms and no provision for re-election to get move responsiveness. One can likewise have long terms for members of parliament in order to get more stability.

B. The Goals

The conservative goal should be referred to as continuity, not as stability. Stability sounds like stagnation. Continuity implies growth, but smooth growth rather than jerky growth. Continuity can imply change, but change in accordance with some kind of predictability based on previously developed trends. The key liberal goal is responsiveness, which is broad enough to include more than just electoral responsiveness. This could be an example of raising one's goals so as to broaden the notion of responsiveness like broadening the notion of unemployment, and also broadening the notion of continuity.

C. The Super-Optimum Solution

The SOS is to say that the structure is not especially important as to whether one has a chief executive who is chosen directly by the people, or indirectly by the people through the parliament. What is needed is a constitutional or statutory commitment on the part of the chief executive and the government in general to a special kind of responsiveness and stability.

1. Responsiveness

A responsiveness that goes beyond merely reading the public opinion polls in order to get re-elected. Responsiveness in the traditional political context has meant that it is easy to throw the government out of power. That is more a process designed to bring about responsiveness than responsiveness in itself. Responsiveness should mean such things as that the government is sensitive to people who are displaced as a result of new technologies or reduced tariffs, i.e. the government is responsive to their need for new jobs. A government is much more responsive if it sees to it that displaced workers find new jobs even though the president is a president for life and cannot be thrown out of office than would be a government in which the prime minister can be replaced by 10% of the parliament saying they want to get rid of him. Responsiveness should mean that when people are hurting, the government does something about it other than changing prime ministers.

2. Stability

On the matter of stability, we do not want stability. We want continuity. We want continuous growth. Growth is change, not stability. We want statutes and constitutional provisions that will require the government, regardless whether it consists of Republicans or Democrats, to engage in policies that guarantee about 6% growth per year. We do have a 1946 Employment Act and a 1970 Humphrey-Hawkins Act that say unemployment should not get above 3%, or that inflation should not get above 3%. Such laws mean nothing because they provide no provision for enforcement. Worse, they provide no provision to achieve those goals. They are the same kind of fiat like King Canute asking the waves to stop, which can be done by the Army Corps of Engineers building appropriate dams, but not simply by issuing a "there shalt not be" statement.

D. A Pair of Constitutional Provisos

The SOS thus would be a set of statutes or a pair of statutes (or better yet, a pair of constitutional provisions).

1. Continuous Economic Growth

That would require 6% a year continuous growth. That is a minimum. There is nothing wrong with doing better than that, even if it is jerky like one year 10%, another year 6%, another year 12%. That sounds very unstable, but neither conservatives nor liberals would object to that kind of instability. Nobody is likely to object to having their income be highly unstable with one year $1 million, the next year $20 million. When people talk about instability they mean jumping from positive to negative, or positive to zero, but not from very high positive to positive and back.

2. Upgrading Skills

The second statute or constitutional right is an obligation to displaced workers to be retrained, relocated. This is like two new constitutional rights. Traditional constitutional rights have related to free speech, equal protection, and due process. Modern constitutional rights have related to social security, minimum wage, safe workplace, and more recently clean air. What we are proposing is a constitutional right to economic growth and to be relocated if one is a displaced worker. The word relocated sounds too much like moving a person from one city to another. We are also talking about upgrading skills so one can get a better job without moving to another city. Instead of talking about the right to relocation, we should talk about the right to upgraded work. It is not the right to work. That phrase has been ruined by people who use it to mean the right not to be in a union. A problem with the concept of the right to upgraded work is there is nothing in that concept that confines it to displaced workers, although that is not necessarily bad. Perhaps all workers should have a right to upgraded work. But especially those who have no work at all as a result of technological change or tariff reductions. If there were really meaningful rights to economic growth and upgraded work, that kind of SOS would score high on continuity. To emphasize that, we need to talk about continuous economic growth. The upgraded work part especially relates to the responsiveness.

E. Making Those Rights Meaningful

A key point is that those rights are not meaningful by merely being stated in statutes or constitutions. They are also not that meaningful by saying that someone who feels he has been denied one of those rights can sue Congress or the president. They are made meaningful by establishing institutions like the Ministry of International Trade and Industry that has a mandate, a budget, personnel, and sub-units that are meaningfully relevant to promoting continuous economic growth. One could establish a separate government agency to enforce the right to upgraded work. The rights become meaningful when you have institutions in place to enforce them, not just words in place in a statute or a constitution. The courts cannot enforce them. It requires specialized administrative agencies. The courts can enforce due process by reversing convictions that violate due process. The courts can enforce free speech and equal protection by issuing injunctions ordering the police to cease interfering with speakers or marchers, or ordering the schools to cease operating segregated classrooms. The courts have no power to award well-targeted subsidies or tax breaks which are needed for economic growth and upgraded work. That requires appropriate administrative agencies.

Chapter 6

INTERNATIONAL POLICY CONTROVERSIES

I. APPLYING SUPER-OPTIMIZING ANALYSIS TO THE PERSIAN GULF CRISIS

A. August 3, 1990

1. Possible Solution

One interesting (possibly even super-optimum solution) is for the U.S., the Arab countries, or a larger grouping of countries to suggest that if Iraq will withdraw from Kuwait, then Israel will withdraw from the occupied territories. What follows was dictated the day after Iraq invaded Kuwait, except for the updating section at the end (See Table 6.1).

2. Incentives to Comply

If Saddam Hussein refused to go along with that, then he would be looked upon as a bad Arab by the Arabs. He could enable the Palestinians to get statehood by his merely withdrawing from someplace where he does not have a legal right to be in the first place. It enables Saddam Hussein to look good in that he is helping the Arab world and the Palestinians, and not being forced out.

If Israel refuses to go along with that, then Israel would look bad in that Israel would be jeopardizing the peace of the whole world. It would be doing so to retain land to which it has no legal right, and to which it never really has claimed a legal right. Israel refers to the area to some extent as occupied territories. There are people in Israel who refer to those territories as being part of Israel. Even they are reluctant to do so because it would mean that if the territories are part of Israel, then the people who live there would have rights that they do not have. This could give Israel an opportunity to look good by giving up the land under circumstances where it is not forced out of them and where Israel is helping the world.

Table 6.1 Persian Gulf Crisis

GOALS ALTERNATIVES	C 1. Keep oil flowing.	L 1. Avoid loss of life. 2. Preserve peace.
C 1. Military action.	+	-
L 1. Diplomatic action.	-	+
N 1. Compromise (both).	0	0
SOS OR WIN-WIN 1. Iraq returns Kuwait. 2. Israel returns occupied territories.	++	++

3. Big Benefits and Low Costs to Each Side

This kind of trade does not exactly fit the seven ways of arriving at SOS solutions. One could say, though, that it represents big benefits to one side with low costs to the other.

Iraq does not suffer any big out-of-pocket costs by withdrawing from Kuwait. One could say they suffer opportunity costs in the sense that if they stay there, maybe they could absorb Kuwait's oil. That may not be too likely, though. Even by withdrawing, they may be losing virtually nothing since they would have lost Kuwait's oil anyhow possibly. President Bush has said he will not tolerate Iraq using Kuwait's oil, and could maybe enforce that without military action by simply boycotting and establishing a blockade to prevent Iraq from exporting the oil.

Israel does not suffer any cost. In fact, they save money by getting rid of the expense they are suffering as a result of trying to keep down the occupied territories.

Iraq gets benefit in the eyes of the Arab world and the world in general. Israel gets benefit in the eyes of the world in general and an opportunity to somewhat redeem itself. The world especially gets benefit by defusing the situation and thereby preventing military action that could result in the loss of a lot of lives. The world also benefits in the sense the oil begins flowing again, which is good for the world economy, including Japan and the United States.

4. Dispute Resolution without Direct Negotiation

This is not an example of dispute resolution between Israel and Iraq that would involve any negotiation between those two countries. Israel could give up the occupied territories, and Iraq could simultaneously give up Kuwait without having any interaction between those two countries. That non-interaction should be to their mutual liking since neither of them is on speaking terms with the other, and they would lose face by even offering to negotiate.

B. January 9, 1991

1. Possible Solution

It looks more and more as if that is going to be the solution reached. The EEC is coming out strongly in favor of it, along with France. But not England. Iraq wants possibly a linkage conference before a withdrawal. The U.S. wants withdrawal before a linkage conference. The logical compromise, which would also be a SOS, would be to have them simultaneously, which is what Miterrand advocates.

Both sides could consider themselves as having won with that kind of outcome. The U.S. can say that it did not yield on linkage before the withdrawal, and Iraq can say it did not withdraw before getting linkage. They can both in the traditional way console themselves by saying that they came out ahead of their worst expectations, or at least out ahead of what the other side wanted.

2. Interferences

That may be clearly the rational way to go in terms of everybody coming out ahead of their best initial expectations. That may not be what will happen, though, because of the various kinds of factors that interfere with adopting or implementing SOS solutions.

A wimp wants to show that he is a toughie. Especially on the side of Bush since nobody has called Saddam Hussein a wimp. Instead, he is called a vicious butcher. It is hard to be a vicious butcher and a wimp simultaneously. What one has to somehow get across is that the simultaneous conference was achieved by macho assembling of 400,000 troops, and without that display of macho bravado it would not have occurred. It proves that being tough is the way to go.

Setting ultimatums can always interfere with arriving at super-optimum solutions. Super-optimum solutions may take more time to develop than ordinary solutions. If one sets an ultimatum for a point in time that does not allow sufficient time, then that can clearly mess up the adoption and implementation. In that context it is important to emphasize that there has been some language on Bush's part that he is not going to be hastily pushed into a war, that his January 15 deadline means that he is ready, willing. and able to go to war on January 15, but that he does not have to if he does not want to. He can also claim new information, such as grasping at whatever sign of not wanting to be invaded that Saddam Hussein sends out, or does not send out.

Things can also get messed up by third parties even if the main parties of Iraq and the U.S. are approaching an SOS or a traditional compromise. Israel might be the most likely to disrupt things, although they have been maintaining a low profile. Israel, though, could be deliberately provoked by an extremist Palestinian group that wants to see a war that will involve Iraq attacking Israel either because the group is so extremist that they would rather be dead than not have their sovereignty, or simply because they think that such a war will lead to obtaining sovereignty.

C. January 17, 1991

1 The Possibilities for a Conference

The possibility of the conference for withdrawal SOS has increased. If the U.S. agrees to a conference now it will not be because we have been threatened or defeated. We will be agreeing because we think it could be a good thing, rather than because we have somehow lost bargaining power or even decreased it.

The possibility of Saddam Hussein going along with this SOS is also greater. He always was in favor of the conference idea and had indicated that he would be willing to withdraw if it were guaranteed. Thus he really indicated more of a willingness to make concessions. When one side says the other side is not willing to make concessions, as the U.S. has done, meaning Mr. Bush, that generally means the other side is quite willing to make concessions, but we do not like their concessions.

It is important for Saddam's ego, if we are willing to allow him to preserve his ego, for him to be able to say he got something out of his efforts. Even though it looks like he obviously is a loser. The something would be a conference idea, even though it is an idea proposed by many people besides Saddam, including France and the European community, plus the third world, plus even Israel if the conference procedures were to Israel's liking.

2. Obtaining Israel's Participation

On the procedures being to Israel's liking, the demands may be unreasonable. Israel, as in the past, may say that no PLO representatives can attend, although they can be part of the delegation from other countries like Jordan, Syria, Iraq, or even Egypt and north African countries. Thus the PLO may wind up with even more representation that if they were directly represented.

The possibility of giving up land for peace must be a possibility. It can not be ruled out. It is also not a matter of giving up what might be considered Israeli land, instead giving up occupied territory. The conservative party of Israel claims that most of the occupied territory belongs to Israel by virtue of being Biblical Sumeria and Judea. That could be open to negotiation. It could be conceded that Israel does own it. That does not mean Israel can not trade some of it for peace.

3. A Camp David for the Middle East

What we could be doing on a super-optimum solution with regard to the conference that might occur includes the following:

1. The conservative alternative from the American and Israeli viewpoint would in the extreme be to seek to expel Palestine from the West Bank and give it all to Israel.
2. The liberals would establish an independent sovereign state called Palestine which would be a member of the U.N.
3. The neutral position would provide for some kind of big restrictions on foreign policy of a new sovereign state, or would provide that it is to be some kind of a U.N. trust territory.
4. A Camp David-type settlement could be reached where Israel gets tremendous foreign aid benefits from the U.S. in return for going along. So does the PLO, just like Israel, and Egypt. Everyone thereby comes out ahead, including the U.S. The U.S. benefits from no longer having to worry about having to fight in the Middle East, which is highly expensive. It could mean a reduction in the military aid to Israel. There would also be a reduction in military aid to Saudi Arabia and other Arab countries of there can be peace in the Middle East. The U.S. thereby saves a lot of money and potential casualties which would otherwise occur.

D. Broader Implications

1. Comparisons with Vietnam

Factors that put U.S. policy in a more favorable light include (1) an enemy who is an imperialistic bully and a homefront dictator, (2) more world backing, (3) no jungles to hide in, (4) no Soviet or Chinese help.

Factors that are about the same include (1) there is religious conflict in both. In Vietnam it was Buddhist against Christians, especially Catholics. In the Persian Gulf it is Moslems against Christians and Jews. (2) There is dedicated nationalism on the side of the underdog to save their country, but no such spirit on the side of the U.S. (3) Both have anti-colonial elements in the sense of trying to throw out a foreign invader, namely the United States. In both cases the U.S. claims to be there by invitation.

Factors that put U.S. policy in a less favorable light include (1) anti-war activism in the U.S. much earlier, (2) potential embarrassment and demoralization to the U.S. from not being able to defeat a foe that seems weaker than North Vietnam and with the U.S. using much greater fire power, (3) availability of crippling economic sanctions that were not adequately used, (4) availability of the conference alternative which has not been adequately used, and (5) possible negative association with Israel, although that has not yet substantially occurred.

2. Miscellaneous Ideas on the Persian Gulf

When this turns into possibly another Vietnam, then the right wing will say the war was lost because nuclear weapons were not used, just as they said Vietnam was lost because the fire power used against Iraq was not used against North Vietnam. If there is a next war with nuclear weapons and the U.S. in effect loses again, then the right wing will say it is because the doomsday weapon was not used, whatever that is.

The U.S. very much loses the war even when it wins it, if it takes months to do so and there are high casualties. If somebody 20 feet tall weighing 1,000 pounds succeeds in beating up a 2-foot tall person weighing 10 pounds, but the giant is blinded and loses both arms and both legs, most outsiders would say that it was not much of a victory.

One interesting thing is that throughout the Vietnam war the government was saying that there was light at the end of the tunnel and that the war would be over any day now. That seems to be one thing that the government has learned from Vietnam. Nobody is saying anything about lights at the end of the tunnel. Instead they keep cautioning that things may take longer than anticipated. The cautioning though may be an underestimate of how long things may take.

Things would have been much shorter if the embargo had been allowed to continue longer so as to exhaust Iraq's supplies. Iraq probably felt that this was a relatively desirable time to be attacked while their supply level was reasonably up.

It has been suggested that the increased money spent on the Persian Gulf by the U.S. government which is amounting to more than a billion dollars a day is good for the U.S. economy by stimulating spending and jobs. That may be true in a very short-sighted short run. For the long haul of international competitiveness, the United States needs to invest in technological development such a retooling the procedures involved in manufacturing automobiles steel, textiles, chemicals, and other important industries. Not having those funds available for that purpose may substantially wipe out much technological growth that might have otherwise occurred. As a result, Japan and Germany which are spending so little in the Persian Gulf war may turn out to be the big economic winners and the U.S. the big economic loser in the important war of international trade and competitiveness. The sooner the Persian Gulf war is over, possibly through an SOS conference, the sooner the United States can move forward in getting its technology and economy updated and more competitive.

It looks as if the Iraq strategy is to allow the U.S. to completely dominate the skies. They are offering no serious resistance. Their planes are being kept underground or being flown north away from the battle areas. Their strategy seems to be to wait for the land war where their technology and their willingness to die can outdo the Americans who have a similar land technology and less willingness to die. Also it is safer to be in an underground bunker than it is to be out moving above ground in the open desert. Bush would definitely be acting politically smarter by holding back on sending in the troops to do any kind of rooting out until months from now or better yet until a settlement is reached.

So far the fatalities on the U.S. side are slight. They may even be slight on the Iraqi side, or at least not horrendous since the U.S. is sensitive to the bully image of slaughtering civilians. The key point is that there is still time to resolve matters before there really are some heavy fatalities on both sides. That is where the SOS solution might especially come in.[1]

II. BEIJING AND TAIPEI

This section involves applying super-optimum solution analysis to the unification problem. See Table 6.2. Such analysis seeks to find solutions to public policy problems whereby conservatives, liberals, and other major viewpoints all come out ahead of their best initial expectations simultaneously.

Table 6.2 Uniting China

GOALS ALTERNATIVES	C Pro-Taiwan (Capitalism)	L Pro-China (Socialism)
C 1. Nationalist takeover.	+	-
L 1. Communist takeover.	-	+
N 1. Two countries.	0	0
SOS OR WIN-WIN 1. Hong Kong solution. 2. Guandong.	++	++

---

[1] As a matter of April, 1991 hindsight, one can say that the Persian Gulf War teaches at least the one lesson that American foreign policy is better off seeking to export the Bill of Rights, rather than supporting repressive regimes. There probably never would have been a Persian Gulf War and its current undesirable aftermath if it had not been for the support of the United States (1) for the Shah of Iran whose repressive regime brought the Ayatollah Khomeini into power, (2) for Saddam Hussein to fight against Khomeini, (3) for the feudalistic emir of Kuwait and the king of Saudi Arabia to fight against Hussein and possibly their own people, and (4) now resupporting Hussein to keep the pro-Iranian Shiite Moslems and the anti-Turkey Kurds in line. Countries that respect civil liberties turn out to be our best trading partners and allies.

A. Mutually Beneficial Trade

The key factor likely to bring them together is trade which refers to:

1. The mainland is a much bigger potential market than Taiwan is. The mainland has a billion people. Taiwan has less than 100 million, and probably less than 30 million.
2. Taiwan does have some advance technologies at the present time, but if they are going to take advantage of them for bargaining purposes they had better work fast, because Beijing is not slouching around with regard to developing its technical capabilities, especially with regard to computers.
3. Taiwan can serve as a kind of transmission port, somewhat like Hong Kong does. But Taiwan is going to have to get along on better terms with Beijing in order to do that opening.
4. Taiwan probably needs Beijing's market more than Beijing needs Taiwan's technology and marketing capabilities. The mainland will always be far more populous but not less capable on technology and marketing.

B. Common History of Independence from the Chinese Emperors

The key symbolic factor likely to bring them together is the idea of Chinese independence from the emperors under Sun Yat-Sen. He is a revered hero in both places.

1. He is becoming even more revered than he has been in the past on the mainland by virtue of being from Guangzhou which is moving up in status in China. The Sun Yat-Sen University is probably the best university outside of Beijing.
2. He is becoming even more revered on Taiwan as the Chinese nationalists begin to look for new, more lasting her symbols than Chang Kai-Shek whose prestige is going down.
3. Both Mao Zedong and Chiang Kai-Shek were students of Sun Yat-Sen and great admirers of him. One interesting symbolic activity would be to have mainland China and Taiwan participate in a big joint celebration of 1992 which would be the 70th anniversary of the 1912 Sun Yat-Sen revolution overthrowing the emperors. They could do various kinds of joint activities.

One mildly complicating factor is that Mao Zedong chose to announce the independence of China from the Nationalists on October 10, 1949, which was the same date that Sun Yat-Sen announced the independence of China from the emperors. Therefore the Taiwan Chinese do not like the idea of celebrating October 10 because it is associated with their defeat. They also do not like celebrating Sun Yat-Sen's birthday partly on the kind of theory that anybody can be born. That is no great accomplishment. The thing to celebrate is the day on which he did something especially worthwhile. To resolve that problem it may be too late to change the dates.

What it might require doing is considering October 10 as the date in which China in 1912 overthrew domestic emperors and in 1949 overthrew a kind of colonial control. It was not just the Nationalist influence thrown out of China in 1949. It was also the United States, Britain, and France, October 10,1949, could be considered as being the date when China finally won the Boxer Rebellion. The Nationalist Chinese do support the Boxer Rebellion. It was a rebellion against England, the United States, and France for one of the worst examples of colonialism, namely trying to force China to buy drugs from those three countries when China did not want to do so. China did not want to be an addicted country. They were trying to get rid of opium. It is often referred to as part of the opium wars, although they were mainly like international gang wars for controlling the opium trade. The Boxer Rebellion was specifically to get rid of the French, American, and British drug dealers. China lost, though, and the drug dealers continued to force drugs on China and also carved up some spheres of influence which they retained for all practical purposes until 1949. The situation is similar to Ho Chi Minh in Vietnam in that even anti-Communists can support his throwing out the French and to some extent throwing out the Americans. The idea of China for the Chinese should be a common symbolic ground.

A drawback to that, though, is that it would not serve much of a useful purpose to bring Taipei and Beijing together to form some new kind of Chinese xenophobic union in which China would feel antagonistic toward the rest of the world. The object is to join Beijing and Taipei into an economic and political union in which they both welcome foreign trade moving both out and in, and they welcome students primarily moving out. They are not going to be able to attract many foreign students for a long time, although both places try to attract some students from developing nations. Beijing especially tries to attract students from Africa.

C. Alternative Ways of Dealing with the Friction

The conservative alternative is for the Nationalists on Taiwan to conquer the mainland and restore the Nationalist government. That has reached the point of absurdity, but it is the conservative position of a Nationalist takeover. The liberal wing position is the opposite, namely that the Communists from the mainland would take over Taiwan. That possibility seems to have ended in the 1950's, which was the last shelling of Taiwan-owned islands by the mainland. There has been no invasion activity since then and also seems a bit absurd. The neutral position is to just leave things as they are with two separate countries. That is not approved by either side. It is not a compromise that either side accepts as a long run solution, but just as a purely temporary position. Both sides fully agree that Taiwan is a province of China. Neither side accepts the two countries idea. The two countries idea is mainly an American idea, although relatively recent. Actually it was a one-country idea with the Nationalists being the one country until the Nixon administration. Then it became a one-country idea with Beijing being the one country. There never really was a period of more than a few months, and maybe a few days, when we had ambassadors in both places. Beijing would not tolerate any

American ambassadors coming there unless they were withdrawn from Taipei. There never was a two-country's approach in a legal sense, only a de facto sense.

The super-optimum solution would involve what both sides want, namely for Taiwan to be recognized as a semi-autonomous province of China like Hong Kong. This would mean the people on Taiwan can consider themselves to be Chinese citizens but at the same time not have Beijing interfere with their capitalistic-oriented economy. Beijing is willing to let provinces on the mainland have that status, such as Guangdong province, and has agreed that should be the status for Hong Kong too. Thus we could say that the super-optimum solution is the Guangdong-Hong Kong solution. Or just the Hong Kong solution. That solution has not been pursued, though, because there has been no meaningful intermediary like there has been in Hong Kong. Britain has served as the intermediary between the Hong Kong Chinese and the mainland Chinese since Britain is the leaseholder on Hong Kong. Britain has served as a kind of mediator and worked out reasonably good terms supported by the majority on both sides. It is not supported by some, particularly on the Hong Kong side who are leaving Hong Kong rather than go along with the agreement. There are some non-supporters on the Beijing side too, who do not like the idea of giving Hong Kong such special status. It does seem a bit much, such as not having to pay any taxes to the national government. No country in the world allows one of its states to be free of paying taxes. If they were willing to do that with Hong Kong, though, they might be with Taiwan. The Beijing government makes a lot of money off of Hong Kong by virtue of the trade without having to collect taxes. The trade that Hong Kong stimulates provides lots of jobs in China for people making products that are sold through Hong Kong.

D. Goals to Be Achieved

As for the goals, the leading conservative goal is to have capitalism prevail. The leading liberal goal is to have socialism prevail.

E. The Hong Kong Solution

The Hong Kong solution provides for both to in effect prevail. Hong Kong is a highly capitalistic place with lots of private enterprise. It also has lots of socialistic government activity. It has been run for years by Great Britain and is about as socialistic as Great Britain is with regard to economic planning and welfare state. There is a need that even conservatives in Hong Kong recognize for more planning in order to keep things from getting too disorganized as a result of immigration and the need for more meaningful zoning given scarce land resources. That is not so much the case with Taiwan. Taiwan is a much bigger territory. It can benefit, though, from the modern form of socialism which is well-placed subsidies and tax breaks, like Japan, Taiwan already does that. That is part of imitating Japan that is done in Korea, Singapore, Taiwan, and for that matter, in Beijing. Thus, what they are getting is private ownership with lots of governmental stimulation in the form of well-placed subsidies and tax breaks.

One could even say a national takeover would not be so conducive to competitive capitalism. It would be monopolistic capitalism. Likewise, a Communist takeover would not be so conducive to socialism in the democratic socialism sense, which is the more modern kind of socialism. A Nationalist takeover would mean non-democratic, uncompetitive capitalism. A Communist takeover would mean non-democratic, noncompetitive socialism. Thus the Hong Kong-Guangdong solution in a way does better on both capitalism and socialism.

III. AMERICAN MILITARY BASES

Developing nations may not be as involved with private international law as more industrialized nations are. Private international law refers to the rules governing business transactions that involve citizens or key facts from different countries. Developing nations may have more need for public international law than developed nations do. Public international law refers to the rules concerning government-to-government relations. The more industrialized countries may be able to resolve their disputes through negotiation without resorting to an international tribunal. The less developed countries with less bargaining power may have more need for international tribunals, as was the case in Nicaragua obtaining an injunction from the International Court of Justice against the mining of its harbors by the United States.

Developing nations may also have international law problems with former colonial powers seeking to maintain a possibly unwanted military presence in the new nation. This is partly the case with the American military bases in the Philippines. The legal and policy problems of those bases may be a fitting way to conclude this paper since they are especially challenging problems, although so are the other previously discussed problems. All these problems in order to qualify as SOS problems need to have the following characteristics:

1. There should be at least one conservative alternative and at least one liberal alternative. If there is only one alternative for dealing with the problem, then there is no problem since there is no choice, although one could say that there is still a go/no-go choice as to whether that one alternative should be adopted.
2. There should be at least one conservative and at least one liberal goal. If all the goals are conservative, then the conservative alternative should easily win. Likewise if all the goals are liberal, then the liberal alternative should easily win,
3. The conservative alternative should do better on the conservative goal, with the liberal alternative doing better on the liberal goal. That is the tradeoff requirement. If either alternative does better on both kinds of goals, then that alternative should easily win.
4. It should be possible to meaningfully say that conservatives give relatively more weight to the conservative goals and relatively less weight to the liberal goals, and vice versa for the assigning of weights by liberals. If that is not so, then it is

not so meaningful to talk about a conservative total with conservative weights and a liberal total with liberal weights.

5. There should be a super-optimum solution that does better than the previous conservative alternative on the conservative totals with conservative weights, and it also does better than the previous liberal alternative on the liberal totals with liberal weights. That is the most difficult to achieve of these five characteristics, but still manageable.

The problem of what to do about the American military bases in the Philippines is especially difficult because it goes beyond the usual dilemma of choosing between (1) a liberal alternative that clearly wins with liberal weights, and (2) a conservative alternative that clearly wins with conservative weights. An analysis of Table 6.3 tends to show that the liberal alternative barely squeaks by the conservative and neutral alternatives on the liberal totals, and the conservative alternative barely squeaks by the other two alternatives on the conservative totals. We thus have an even tighter than usual dilemma between the liberal and conservative alternatives.

TABLE 6.3 THE PHILIPPINE-U.S. MILITARY BASES

CRITERIA / ALTERNATIVES	L Goal Liberal Concerns	C Goal Conservative Concerns	L Goal Sovereignty	N Total Neutral weights	L Total Liberal weights	C Total Conservative weights
C Alternative Bases and more money	3	4	2	18	19	17*
L Alternative No bases	3	2	4	18	23*	13
N Alternative Phase out	3	3	2	16	18	14
S Alternative Bases and massive credits to upgrade economy	5	5	3	26	29**	23**

A. The Alternatives

Working backward from those totals to the alternatives, the conservative alter-native is basically to allow the American bases to remain, but to ask for more money. The liberal alternative is to throw the bases out. The neutral alternative is something in between, generally a gradual phasing out of the bases. Other in-between positions might involve throwing out the Clark Air Base but keeping the Subic Naval Base, or vice versa. Another possibility is allow the bases but with more flying of Philippine flags at the bases and other symbols of Philippine sovereignty. A recent middling position is allow the bases, but give the Philippine government more say in how the planes should be used, especially with regard to putting down an attempted coup.

The phasing out idea is probably the most common middling alternative. It, however, blends into both the conservative and the liberal alternatives. The conservatives are willing to tolerate the bases, but they are going to be eventually phased out to some extent anyhow as the cold war decreases even further. They are also going to be phased out to some extent because they have probably already become rather obsolete in light of modern defense technology. Few if any of the planes or ships could ever get anywhere without being destroyed by modern missiles. The Russian equivalent of nuclear-armed Trident submarines in the Pacific Ocean could probably wipe out both the naval base and the air base almost before the alarm could ring. There are also bases that are possibly more welcome in nearby Okinawa and Korea.

Likewise, the liberal alternative of throwing out the bases would have to be phased out. They cannot be thrown out within a matter of hours. For one thing, the liberal and conservative members of the Philippine House of Representatives would not tolerate a rushed departure without allowing for substitute employment opportunities and some substitution for the large amounts of money that are spent by Americans associated with the bases. The Philippine Senate is elected at large and is not so sensitive to Luzon constituency pressures where the bases are located.

One might therefore think there is really only one alternative here, namely phase out the bases. This problem, however, illustrates the importance of symbolism and language in political controversy. Whether the liberals really mean it or not, they talk about throwing out the bases now, not phasing them out. Whether the conservatives really mean it or not, they talk about retaining the bases indefinitely. Thus the controversy needs to be resolved in terms of what each side argues, not necessarily in terms of the realities beneath the surface. Perceptions, value judgments, and symbolism are often more important in resolving political controversies than empirical reality, especially in the short run.

B. The Goals

As for goals, Table 6.3 lists the first goal as "Liberal Concerns." That means a whole set of interests that liberals are especially sensitive to, including workers rather than employers, consumers rather than merchants, tenants rather than landlords, small farmers-businesses rather than big farmers-businesses, debtors rather than creditors, minority ethnic groups rather than dominant ethnic groups, and in general the relatively less well-off segments within society. The second goal is listed as "Conservative Concerns." That means a set of interests to which conservatives are especially sensitive, including employers, merchants, landlords, big farmers, big businesses, creditors, and dominant ethnic groups. One useful aspect of this problem is that it goes to the heart of liberal versus conservative interests and constituencies, as contrasted to lower impact problems.

The third goal is national sovereignty. In some contexts, that can be a conservative goal such as where Russia nationalists talk about restraining the Lithuanians, expelling the Jews, or otherwise discriminating against citizens of the Soviet Union who are not ethnic Russians. In other contexts, sovereignty can be a liberal left-wing goal, such as where Vietnamese advocate becoming sovereign from China, France, Japan, France again, the United States, and China again during various points in Vietnamese history. Likewise it is a liberal concept in the Philippines when Filipinos talk about getting rid of the Spanish colonialists or the American Imperialists. including what they consider to be military-base imperialism. That makes sovereignty in this analysis a relatively liberal goal. Obviously the goal of conservative concerns is a conservative goal, and the goal of liberal concerns is a liberal one.

C. Scoring the Relations

As for scoring the relations of the alternatives on the goals, both the liberal and conservative concerns are to some extent favorably benefited by the present and additional American dollars. Those dollars benefit both workers and employers, consumers and merchants, tenants and landlords, small and large farmers, small and large businesses, debtors and creditors, and both minority and dominant ethnic groups. The amount of money is quite substantial. The Philippines is one of the top three recipients of American foreign aid in the world along with Israel and Egypt, whose aid is lessening. The liberal and conservative concerns, however, do not benefit equally. The American presence has a conservative influence. The United States tends to be supportive of conservative pro-American politicians, especially in a country that has American military bases like Korea, Greece, Turkey, West Germany, Spain, and the Philippines.

To be more specific, the conservative alternative of retaining the bases with even more money is a bit of a wash or a 3 on a 1-5 scale with regard to liberal concerns. The money is at least a 4 on liberal concerns, but the conservative influence of the United States is a 2 or lower. Those two sub-scores average a 3. On the conservative concerns, the conservative alternative of the bases and more money gets at least a 4 On sovereignty, the conservative alternative is at least a 2 on a 1-5 scale, which is the equivalent of a -1 on a -1 to +2 scale.

The liberal alternative also produces a washed-out 3 on liberal concerns. It gets a 4 with regard to getting rid of some of the American conservative influence, but it gets a 2 on losing the American money. The liberal alternative of no bases gets a 2 or lower on conservative concerns. It does relatively well on sovereignty, as both liberals and conservatives can recognize, although they may disagree on the relative weight of sovereignty in this context.

The neutral phase-out approach does about middling on liberal concerns. It provides some money for a while, which is good, but not as good as a lot of money for a long time. It provides a diminishing of American conservative Influence, but not as fast as the liberals would like, and not as slow as the conservatives might like. By allowing the Americans to retain the bases even under a phase-out arrangement, the neutral alternative does have a negative effect on Philippine sovereignty, although not as negative as the conservative alternative. We could show that difference by giving the neutral alternative a 2.5 on sovereignty or the conservative alternative a 1.5. Either way, the overall results are not affected.

D. A Super-Optimum Solution

Those overall results are that the liberal alternative wins on the liberal totals and the conservative alternative wins on the conservative totals although not by much, as previously mentioned. Finding a super-optimum solution may be especially difficult where the alternatives are so nearly tied and where the problem is so filled with emotional symbolism. A possible super-optimum solution would involve two key elements. The first is a recognition (as much as possible on all sides) that the bases are probably going to be phased out in the future. This will not be due to the United States surrendering or to the Philippines overcoming the U.S. opposition. It will be more due to defense technology changes (as mentioned above) that makes these bases about as meaningful as the Maginot Line in France in 1940, Pearl Harbor in the United States in 1941, or the Singapore guns pointing to the sea in 1942. The phasing out will also be due to recent world changes that seem to greatly decrease the likelihood of a world war between the Soviet Union, Eastern Europe, and China on the one hand, and the United States and its allies on the other hand.

More important than a natural rather than a forced phase-out is a second key element of a possible super-optimum solution. This element emphasizes massive credits to upgrade the Philippine economy. It could involve no payment of cash whatsoever on the part of the United States and yet provide tremendous economic benefits to the Republic of the Philippines. It involves a number of characteristics. First of all, the United States makes available an amount of credits that when expressed in dollars would be about twice as many dollars as the United States would be willing to pay In the form of rent or a cash payment. The United States would be willing to pay more in the form of credits because:

1. It is normally a lot easier to give credit than to pay cash. An example might be returning merchandise to a store and asking for cash. One may receive various negative reactions as to why the merchandise should be kept. If, however, one asks for a credit slip, the decision-maker is likely to be much more accommodating.
2. The American economy would substantially benefit if the credits could only be used in the United States to buy American products and services. That would benefit the United States more than paying out cash that then gets spent in Japan or elsewhere. At the same time, it does not substantially hamper the Philippines in buying products and services needed for upgrading its economy.
3. The U.S. economy would also substantially benefit indirectly from an upgrading of the Philippine economy, since that would enable the Philippines to buy even more American products and services in the future.

As for what the credits would be for, that is where the Philippines could especially benefit. The shopping list might include such things as:

1. Credits to pay for personnel and facilities for on-the-job training and adult education to upgrade worker productivity.
2. Relevant credits for upgrading Philippine higher education, especially in fields that relate to engineering and public policy which could have high marginal rates of return.
3. Relevant credits for upgrading elementary and secondary education as part of a large-scale investment in human resource development.
4. Relevant credits for seeds, pesticides, herbicides, and farm equipment to make the previously mentioned land reform programs more successful, including the hiring of experts for training programs.
5. Relevant credits for subsidizing suburban job opportunities, regional cities, and overseas employment opportunities.
6. Relevant credits to improve energy and electricity production in the Philippines which is such an important aspect of improving the gross national product.
7. Relevant credits for buying technologies that can improve productivity along with upgraded skills, including modern assembly line technologies.
8. Relevant credits for health care and housing that can be shown to be related to increased worker productivity.
9. Other credits for buying American products and services that relate to upgrading the Philippine economy, as contrasted to buying consumer goods or other products and services that have little increased productivity payoff.

There are additional benefits for both sides that should be mentioned. By both sides in this context is meant the Republic of the Philippines and the United States. Both sides also refers to the liberals and conservatives within the Philippines. Some additional features are:

1. By providing credits rather than cash, there is a minimum of loss due to corruption. It is a lot easier to pocket money than it is to pocket a new schoolhouse or an expert consultant in on-the-job training.

2. By providing credits that are earmarked for upgrading the economy, there is a minimum of loss due to wasteful expenditures including bureaucratic administration.

3. Waste is not going to be completely eliminated. We would not want a straitjacket system that discourages experimentation with innovative ideas for increasing productivity. If innovation is going to be encouraged, some waste must be expected since not all innovative ideas work out well.

4. This could set a precedent for future American aid to other countries and future aid by other developed countries to developing countries. The key aspect of the precedent is emphasizing credits for upgrading the economy, as contrasted to an emphasis on food, shelter, clothing, and other traditional charitable do-gooderism.

5. In that regard, we are talking about teaching people how to fish, rather than giving them a fish. The fishing analogy is endorsed by liberals who founded the Peace Corps and conservatives who believe in workfare rather than charitable handouts. Actually we are talking about teaching people how to develop and apply new technologies for doing such things as fishing, growing crops, manufacturing products, transporting commuters, and making public policy decisions.

6. The kind of program that most wins friends and influences people in favor of the United States might be programs that involve bringing left-wing anti-Americans to the United States to receive training or having American trainers go to work with Philippine union leaders or Mindinao farmers. People acquire a much more favorable attitude toward Americans in that context than by receiving a sack of flour labeled Made in the U.S.A.

It might be noted that if the Filipinos emphasize how obsolete the bases are becoming, they might succeed in getting rid of the bases faster. On the other hand, it might be wise to emphasize how valuable the bases are in order to get even more credits as payment for retaining them. On the third hand, the United States is not so unaware of the empirical realities, and it is not so unaware of bargaining techniques. This idea of retaining the bases along with an inevitable at least partial phase-out and massive credits for upgrading the Philippine economy should not be approached as a matter of traditional negotiation and game playing. Rather it should be approached as a matter that can be resolved to the mutual benefits of all sides in the sense of a super-optimum solution with all major viewpoints coming out ahead of their initial best expectations. Also see Table 6.4 "Simplified Table on Philippine-U.S."

Table 6.4 Simplified Table On Philippine-U.S. Military Bases

GOALS / ALTERNATIVES	C 1. Conservative concerns.	L 1. Liberal concerns. 2. Sovereignty.
C Bases and more money.	+	-
L No bases.	-	+
N Phase out.	0	0
SOS OR WIN-WIN Bases and massive credits to upgrade economy.	++	++

IV. THE ISRAELI CONTROVERSY

Four types of Jews can be characterized by giving them names. See Table 6.5. That de-emphasizes the emotionality and adds a touch of humor:

1. Rabbi Rabinowich is the traditional pious Jew. Very untough. Contributes to charity.
2. Sgt. Rambowitz. Very tough. Does not contribute to charity. Thinks beggars are weak people.
3. Professor Rabin. He or she has changed his name in order to become an ivy league professor.
4. Captain Marowitz who is the Jewish version of Captain Marvel. He is tough but not a bully. He seeks to rescue people from bullies. He is more of a do-gooder than the pious Jew who puts money into the beggar's cup. Captain Marowitz risks his life to parachute behind enemy lines to open the gates of a concentration camp.

How they score on the two goals of toughness and altruism:

1. The pious rabbinical student may do well with regard to one-on-one altruism, but is untough, and his altruism does not produce any big consequences.
2. The military Jew is tough, but not very oriented toward doing any good in the sense of helping people, let alone saving the world.

3. The professor may be intellectually tough, but not physically. He may discover a Salk vaccine which is definitely helpful to the world, but does not involve any personal risk. There is no great danger in working in a lab, although in the case of the Curies, working with cancer-causing radium was dangerous but unknown to them. In order to do an act of bravery, one has to be aware that one is doing something dangerous.

4. The SOS combines well both toughness in the sense of taking physical risks and at the same time having important consequences. They are not physical risks that involve mountain climbing. They are physical risks that involve going into a black ghetto environment to defuse a riot. Going into a place like Sarajevo in order to try to open up an airport or road for a relief convoy.

Table 6.5 Jewishness

GOALS ALTERNATIVES	C Toughness.	L Altruism.
C Military (Sgt. Rambowitz).	+	-
L Traditional (Rabbi Rabinowich).	-	+
N Intellectual (Professor Rabin).	0	0
SOS OR WIN-WIN SOS. (Capt. Marowitz).	++	++

The closest thing to Captain Marowitz in Jewish literature may be the early novels of Leon Uris like Exodus and Mila 17. The hero of Exodus is Ari Ben-Canaan. The hero of Mila 17 is a boy from the Warsaw ghetto.

This is an analysis of different notions of Jewishness, not an analysis of different ways of resolving the Arab-Israeli conflict, although it could be translated into those terms.

1. The ultra-orthodox Jew would relate to Arabs the way they have for over 2,000 years from the time of the Roman Empire until the 1900s. The relation was one of submissiveness. To a considerable extent, the Jews in old Palestine lived by taking in each other's charity. Each beggar gave to the other beggar.

2. The military solution is conquest and expulsion.

3. The intellectual solution is discussion, analysis, and debate, which can go on interminably.

4. The SOS for Captain Marowitz involves altruistic acts of heroism, possibly risking his life to save an Arab who is being bullied by an Israeli soldier. On a larger scale, he arranges a meeting with Al Fatah extremists to try to convince them with partly physical means to lay off on their emphasis on terrorism and assassinations. He risks his life to grab a terrorist bomb that was thrown on a bus in order to carry it off the bus. The key thing is he risks his life to save either Arabs or Jews who are being subjected to life-threatening circumstances and who are not military people, but basically innocent civilians. There are Israelis like that and American Jews who have gone to Israel who are like that. The problem is that the Captain Marowitz syndrome in the past has overemphasized almost supernatural abilities like those of Captain Marvel. This has made it a kind of daydream fiction.

The reality of the present is that one can do a lot more for reducing Israeli terrorism or Arab terrorism through actively working on behalf of international dispute resolution. That can include such things as developing a published symposium consisting of insightful analyses by professors from Arab, Israeli, and other universities, writing on how they perceive the situation could be substantially improved. The object is not only to get such insightful analyses written, but to get them widely dispersed into the reading of key decision-makers. That kind of activity could have major consequences. It could involve a great deal of hard work and perseverance and maybe some physical dangers. But mainly, the toughness that is associated with persevering against what others would consider to be an impossible challenge.

V. USIS WIN-WIN TRAVELING SEMINARS

Regarding the USIS traveling seminars dealing with conflict resolution in South Asia and elsewhere, the key *general ideas* are:

1. The world can be divided into the five continents of Africa, Asia, Europe, Latin America, and North America. Each continent can then be divided into approximately six regions sharing a common geography and possibly a common language or culture. Appendix 1 roughly divides the developing world into 24 regions for the purpose of conducting workshops or traveling seminars.

2. Each traveling seminar can include a leading authority from each country within the region. Those authorities will generally be professors teaching political or social science since those are the issues to be emphasized. The authorities can be referred to as the presenters since each seminar will begin with their brief presentations.

3. The traveling seminar can spend at least one day in each country within each region. The roundtable participants or discussants can consist of leading academics, journalists, and government people from the country or countries where the traveling seminars occur.
4. The topic of each traveling seminar will be approximately "U.S. Policy with _____ in the 90's and Beyond," with the name of the region inserted.
5. A key purpose of the seminar will be to clarify how policies can be developed that are mutually beneficial between the United States and the countries of the region. Such policies can also be developed between countries and groups within the region, and also with international organizations that involve the region.
6. This mutuality purpose will draw upon ideas form win-win dispute resolution, super-optimizing policy analysis, and related conflict resolution ideas. The moderator for the traveling seminars should be someone well versed and experienced in such methods, but not one who is considered an authority on the region.

A. Format, Implementation, and Feedback

The general format involves the following steps:

1. Opening remarks from the USIS and the moderator.
2. Brief presentations from the authorities addressed to the topic of the seminar. Allow for a total of about 120 minutes. Each speakers gets 120/N minutes where N is the number of speakers.
3. The moderator summarizes the points of agreement and disagreement among the presenters.
4. The participants raise questions and make comments for at least 60 minutes before breaking for lunch.
5. The presenters then offer a reappraisal of their original presentations in light of the questions and comments that have been raised. Allow for a total of about 60 minutes. Each speaker gets 60/N minutes.
6. Allow at least 60 minutes of further questions and comments in light of the reappraisals.
7. The moderator summarizes new points of agreement and disagreement. The moderator also provides integration and comments concerning procedures for possibly resolving the points of disagreement.
8. The presenters and discussants react to the moderator's summary with further questions, comments, suggestions, and rebuttal.
9. The USIS host says a few parting words followed by a cocktail reception.

As for the implementation of these substantive ideas in South Asia, Appendix 2 contains the following relevant items:

1. A copy of the agenda for the traveling seminar that was held in Bombay.
2. A causal arrow diagram entitled "U.S. Policy and Economic, Political, and Military Matters in Developing and Industrialized Nations." It was used to summarize the morning presentations and discussion.
3. An international flow chart entitled "U.S. Policy Over Time Toward Developing and Industrialized Nations." It was used to summarize the afternoon reappraisals and discussion.

As for the implementation of these procedural ideas in South Asia, Appendix 3 contains the following relevant items:

1. A short article on "Super-Optimizing Analysis and Policy Studies" from the *Policy Studies Journal*.
2. An application of those ideas to the economic problem of "Trade Versus Aid in South Asia and Elsewhere."
3. An application to the political problem of "Secession in South Asia and Elsewhere."
4. An application to the military problem of "Having Nuclear Weapons in South Asia and Elsewhere."

The *feedback* for the three traveling seminars conducted in New Delhi, Sri Lanka, and Bombay has been quite favorable:

1. The USIS persons who most actively participated in the three seminars all praised them. They included Richard Scorza of New Delhi, William Maurer of Sri Lanka, and Roger Rosco of Bombay.
2. The presenters also indicated they were quite pleased at the farewell dinner which was held in Bombay. The presenters included Professor Pervais Cheema of Pakistan, Shelton Kodikara of Sri Lanka, and S.D. Muni of India.
3. The seminar also received favorable comments from the participants in all three places. Those comments referred to the conflict resolution purposes of the seminar as well as the South Asia substance.

B. Win-Win U.S. Foreign Policy

The leading controversial issues in developing nations like those of South Asia tend to be economic, political, and military issues. (1) The economic issues relate to how to make domestic economies more prosperous and how to facilitate investments, exports, and imports. (2) The political issues relate to promoting democratic institutions, human rights, and self-determination. (3) The military issues relate to nonproliferation of arms and reduction in regional conflicts.

The first six causal relations in Table 6.6 can be interpreted as follows: (1) Reduction in military conflicts is conducive to prosperity and investment, (2) Prosperity is conducive to reduction in military conflicts, especially prosperity based on buying and selling across countries that might otherwise be in conflict, (3) Prosperity is conducive to democratic institutions, human rights, and tolerance of minority ethnic groups, (4) Democracy, human rights, and ethnic peace are conducive to prosperity, (5) Democratic political institutions are also conducive to a reduction in military conflicts, and (6) Reducing military conflicts is also conducive to democratic political institutions.

TABLE 6.6 WIN-WIN U.S. FOREIGN POLICY

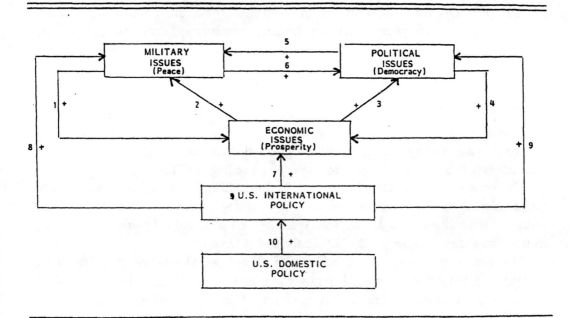

The last four causal relations can be interpreted as follows: (7) U.S. policy is concerned with encouraging prosperity, investment, exporting, and importing because doing so is mutually beneficial, (8) U.S. policy is concerned with reducing military conflicts partly because of the favorable effect on prosperity and the economic issues, (9) U.S. policy is concerned with promoting a democratic political environment partly because of the favorable effect on prosperity and the economic issues, and (10) U.S. domestic economic policy emphasizes U.S. prosperity and GNP growth which partly explains why U.S. international policy emphasizes mutually beneficial trade and investment opportunities.

Miscellaneous points: (1) In the context of South Asia, Pakistan is especially concerned with military security; India is especially concerned with political issues; Sri Lanka is especially concerned with international economics; but all three countries are concerned with all three sets of issues. (2) The concept of mutual benefit is promoted through regional organizations, such as the South Asia Association for Regional Cooperation as well as through interregional interaction between South Asia and the U.S. (3) Social issues are also important such as poverty and ethnic groups, although they were considered under economic and political issues, respectively. Technology issues are also quite important, but they were discussed in the context of military, economic, and political issues. (4) There are positive relations among all five variables shown in Table 1. Those relations are positive in the sense of upward causation and being desirable relations, especially regarding promotion of peace, prosperity and democracy.

C. Past U.S. Foreign Policy

The past was characterized by colonialism and the Cold War. The present is being characterized by investment, importing, and exporting of funds and foods. The future may be characterized by transfer of technologies and skills from the U.S. which results in mutually beneficial investment-returns, buying, and selling. See Table 6.7.

The arrows from the past indicate: (1 & 2) Colonialism involved low wages going to the developing nations, and valuable resources going to the United States or other industrialized nations. (3 & 4) The Cold War involved arms and aid going to developing nations and allegiance going to the U.S. or the Soviet Union.

The arrows from the present indicate: (5 & 6) Capital investment going to the developing nations with a reasonable return going back to the United States. (7 & 8) Cash or credits going to developing nations in return for their products. (9 & 10) Products going to developing nations in return for their cash or credits.

The arrows from the future indicate: (11 &12) Technologies and skill go to developing nations thereby improving their ability to be good places for investment, buying, and selling.

In the past, there was often an imbalance with disproportionate benefits to the industrial nations and disproportionate detriments to the developing nations. In the present, there is generally mutual benefits form investment, exporting, and importing. In the future, the transfer of technologies and skills may enable all participating countries to exceed their best initial expectations simultaneously.

TABLE 6.7 U.S. FOREIGN POLICY FOR 200 YEARS

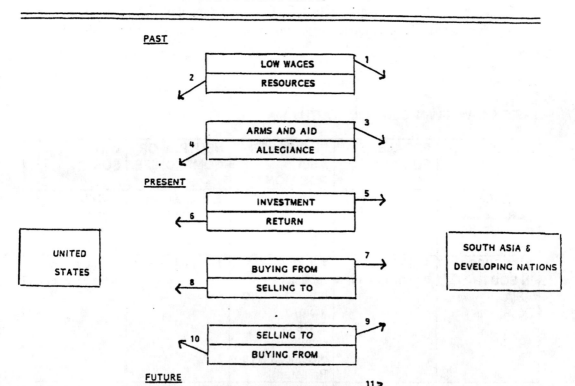

C. Win-Win Issues in South Asia (See Table 6.8)

1. Trade versus Aid

The U.S. currently tends to favor trade over aid, since trade is more mutually beneficial than aid which tends to mainly benefit the recipient nation unless there is a Cold War return.

Developing nations tend to favor aid with no strings attached at least in the past, since they are fearful that (1) buying from the United States will disrupt local industries, and that (2) they have little to sell the United States.

Skills and technology transfer greatly benefit the United States by virtue of improving places for (1) U.S. investment, (2) the buying of American products, and (3) selling to the U.S. products needed by the American people.

Skills and technology transfer benefit developing nations by enabling them to upgrade their international competitiveness even more than offering them either trade or aid.

TABLE 6.8 WIN-WIN ISSUES IN SOUTH ASIA

ISSUES	PRO-U.S. POSITION	PRO-SOUTH ASIA POSITION	NEUTRAL OR COMPROMISE	WIN-WIN OR SOS
1. TRADE VERSUS AID IN SOUTH ASIA	1. Mainly trade	1. Mainly aid	1. Some trade 2. Some aid	1. Skills transfer 2. Technology transfer
2. SECESSION IN SOUTH ASIA (KASHMIR)	1. Self-determination	1. Retain rebellious provinces (Pro-India) 2. Release rebellious provinces (Pro-Pakistan)'	1. Partition	1. Autonomy like a U.S. state
3. NUCLEAR ARMS IN SOUTH ASIA	1. No nuclear arms	1. Retain the capability that exists	1. Reduce 2. Inspect	1. Peaceful conversion

2. Seceding

The U.S. tends to favor self-determination out of a regard for democratic decision-making and emphasizing the majority will within the rebellious provinces.

Developing nations tend to favor retaining their own rebellious provinces, emphasizing the majority will within the larger political entity.

Autonomy like an U.S. state refers to states having their own constitutions and governors that cannot be removed by Washington. States in India do not have their own constitutions and their governors can be removed by New Delhi.

3. Nuclear Arms

The U.S. tends to favor removal of nuclear arms from South Asia for fear that their presence may lead to nuclear warfare which might involve the United States directly or indirectly by way of the international disruption.

Countries which have nuclear capability like India and Pakistan are reluctant to weaken their deterrent power against each other.

Peaceful conversion in this context means providing India and Pakistan with the skills and technologies for converting their nuclear capability into peaceful and safe nuclear energy along with American investment funding.

VI. INTERNATIONAL INTERACTION FOR REGIONAL DEVELOPMENT

A. What the Field Includes

The field of global policy studies can be *defined* as the study of international interactions designed to deal with shared public policy problems.
Such policy problems can include:

1. Trans-boundary problems like people, pollution, or goods literally going across international boundaries.
2. Common property problems like the oceans, Antarctica, or the atmosphere, which nobody owns but are a kind of common good that need to be regulated, expanded, or substituted, or else (like the tragedy of the commons) they will be devoured to the mutual detriment of the nations of the world.
3. Simultaneous problems like health, education, and welfare about which all countries can learn from each other.

B. How the Field Differs from Related Fields

Global policy studies is related to *international relations*, comparative government, and public policy studies. None of those three political science fields, however, is adequately studying the subject of global policy studies. International relations concentrates on relations among countries that relate to diplomacy, alliances, and the resolution of disputes that might otherwise result in war. There are international institutions concerned with public policy studies, such as the specialized agencies of the United Nations, but they are not part of the mainstream of the study of international relations. One might also note that important international interactions associated with global policy studies may not be institutionalized, such as the economic summit meetings, or other even less formal meetings among government officials of various countries designed to deal with shared policy problems.

The field of *comparative* public policy is cross-national in the sense of dealing with a multiplicity of countries. The analysis, however, tends to be one country at a time. Sometimes comparisons are made across countries with an attempt to explain and evaluate differences and similarities. The element of international interaction is, however, missing, which is essential to global policy studies. "Global" does not mean that all countries of the world interact simultaneously, but rather that all countries of the world do share the policy problems under consideration, or at least potentially share them.

The field of *policy studies* tends to concentrate on the single country of the political or social scientist who is working in the field. Some policy studies scholars do look to other countries, but mainly for the purpose of getting ideas that have predictive or prescriptive power within their own countries. They seldom look to international interaction, although they may look at the interaction that occurs between states, provinces, cities, or other sub-national units within their own countries. If each country seeks to maximize its own quality of life without cooperative interaction, the countries in general may suffer important opportunity costs as in other sub-optimizing situations. The classical example is each country trying to produce whatever goods it produces best, and as a result, the world winds up with surpluses and shortages on all goods. It should, however, be noted that in the absence of world government, it will be necessary for individual countries working together by formal or informal agreement to make use of the positive and negative incentives which they have available for encouraging internationally desired behavior.

C. Multiple Dimensions

The field provides good balance on a number of dimensions including theoretical, geographical, purpose, disciplinary, ideological, and methodological.

1. Balance between cross-cutting theoretical matters and those that are more specific in nature. The theoretical orientation, however, is not overly abstract, and the discussion of the specific policy problems does not emphasize anecdotal case studies.

2. Balance among various parts of the world is represented by the researchers in the field including political and social scientists from England, Germany, Poland, India, Spain, the Philippines, and the United States. There is even better balance in terms of the countries that are referred to by the researchers which include all major parts of the world.

3. Balance between prescriptive or evaluative analysis and predictive or explanatory analysis. The field is thus concerned with both (1) explaining variations in the occurrence of international interaction for dealing with shared policy problems and (2) prescribing how such international interaction can be improved to be more effective, efficient, and equitable in achieving its goals.

4. Balance across *disciplinary* perspectives. The researchers in the field are primarily political scientists, but they recognize that one cannot deal adequately with policy problems without bringing in the perspectives of other social sciences and other fields of knowledge, such as economics, sociology, psychology, and natural science.

5. Balance across *ideological* perspectives. The researchers in the field come from a variety of ideological backgrounds in terms of how government should relate to the economy or to the people, and how government should be organized. There may, however, be an underlying pragmatism that is especially associated with policy studies as contrasted to political theory, and a searching for solutions to global policy problems that will be recognized as desirable regardless of

ideology. There may also be an underlying virtual unanimity in favor of an expansion of the elements of democracy that are conducive to academic creativity and interaction, as contrasted to balancing democracy and dictatorship.

6. Balance across *methodological* orientations. This includes studies that emphasize verbal analysis or quantitative analysis. There may, however, be a tendency to get away from unstructured verbal description and make more use of systematic analytic frameworks such as talking in terms of multi-criteria decision-making. Doing so involves analyzing a set of goals to be achieved, alternatives available for achieving them, and relations between goals and alternatives in order to choose or explain the best alternative, combination, allocation, or predictive decision rule. There may also be a tendency to get away from unthinking cross-national quantitative description that involves correlating policy-irrelevant or policy-relevant variables against other variables or each other for 160 members of the United Nations.

D. Current Developments

It is difficult to say when the study of international interaction to deal with shared policy problems first began. One landmark book in the field is Marvin Soroos, *Beyond Sovereignty: The Challenge of Global Sovereignty* (University of South Carolina Press, 1986). Before that, there have been studies of specialized agencies within the United Nations and the League of Nations, including the International Labor Organization, the World Health Organization, and other international agencies concerned with specific policy problems. That earlier literature tended to focus on those semi-governmental institutions rather than on more informal types of interaction. A key volume in the earlier literature is Robert Keohane and Joseph Nye, *Power and Interdependence: World Politics in Transition* (Little, Brown, 1977).

A key event since the Soroos book is the development of the beginnings of a Study Group on "Global Policy Studies" within the International Political Science Association. A petition is now pending for the establishment of such a group. That petition arose as a result of the enthusiasm shown at the 1988 IPSA tri-annual meeting in Washington, D.C. at the global policy studies panels.

During the 1990s, the Global Policy Studies Research Section of the IPSA flourished along with the Developmental Policy Studies Consortium of the Policy Studies Organization. The two groups now publish a quarterly periodical called Developmental Policy Studies, which is completing its fourth volume. The two groups have been sponsoring worldwide workshops dealing with systematic policy studies including win-win analysis. Those workshops have been held in such places Argentina (1991), China (almost every year since 1989), East Africa (1991), Ghana (1987), Korea (1997), Mexico (1997), Middle East (1995), Morocco (1989), Philippines (1990), Russia (1991), South Asia (1992), Thailand (1992), and West Africa (1998), thereby covering the four developing regions of Africa, Asia, East Europe, and Latin America. The groups have also published numerous books, the most important (1) a four-volume set for Macmillan covering the four developing regions, (2) a six-volume set for Marcel Dekker covering economic, technology, social, political, international, and legal policy on a global scale, and (3) various monographs for Ashgate Publishers and JAI Press.

VII. INTERNATIONAL ECONOMIC COMMUNITIES

An exciting new development with regard to international interaction to deal with shared policy problems is the international economic community. It involves a group of countries agreeing to remove tariff barriers to the buying and selling of goods among the countries as a minimum agreement to constitute an IEC. The agreement may also provide for removal of immigration barriers to the free flow of labor, and a removal of whatever barriers might exist to the free flow of communication and ideas. The European Economic Community is a good example, but other examples are developing in North America, Africa, Asia, and East Europe.

Table 6.9 shows how IEC's can be viewed as super-optimum solutions where conservatives, liberals, and other major viewpoints can all come out ahead of their best initial expectations simultaneously. The conservative alternative emphasizes nationalism and separatism. The liberal alternative emphasizes one world or world government. The neutral alternative emphasizes regional government which involves political institutions more than an economic community.

Table 6.9 International Economic Communities

GOALS / ALTERNATIVES	C National identity and stature.	L Quality of life in terms of jobs and consumer goods.
C Nationalism and separatism.	+	-
L One world or world government.	-	+
N Regional government.	0	0
SOS OR WIN-WIN Economic community.	++	++

The conservative goals emphasize national identity and stature. The liberal goals emphasize quality of life in terms of jobs and consumer goods. The conservative alternative does better on the conservative goal as one would expect. The liberal alternative, however, does better on the liberal goal. Thus, the traditional alternatives result in a tradeoff, where the overall winner depends on whether one has conservative goals or liberal goals.

The alternative of having an economic community does well on the conservative goal of preserving national identity since no sovereignty is lost in an IEC, as contrasted to the sovereignty that is lost in a world government or a regional government. The IEC may also add to the national stature of the component parts by giving them the increased strength which comes from being part of an important group. Thus, France may have more national stature as a leader in the European Economic Community than it has alone.

Likewise, the alternative of having an economic community does well on the liberal goal of promoting quality of life in terms of jobs and consumer goals. Jobs are facilitated by the increased exporting that the IEC countries are able to do. Jobs may also be facilitated by free movement to countries in the IEC that have a need for additional labor. Consumer goods are facilitated by the increased importing that the IEC countries are able to do without expensive tariffs.

Thus, the IEC alternative does well on both the conservative goal and the liberal goal. It is therefore able to be a winner on both the liberal totals and the conservative totals. In that sense it has the qualities of a super-optimum solution in the realm of international interaction designed to deal with important economic policy problems.

INDEX

N

O

P